FLORENCE

ENCOUNTE

ROBERT LANDON

Florence Encounter

Published by Lonely Planet Publications Pty Ltd
ABN 36 005 607 983

Australia	Head Office, Locked Bag 1, Footscray, Victoria 3011 ☎ 03-8379 8000 fax 03-8379 8111 talk2us@lonelyplanet.com.au
USA	150 Linden St, Oakland, CA 94607 ☎ 510-250 6400 toll free 800 275 8555 fax 510-893 8572 info@lonelyplanet.com
UK	2nd fl, 186 City Rd, London EC1V 2NT ☎ 020-7106 2100 fax 020-7106 2101 go@lonelyplanet.co.uk

This title was commissioned in Lonely Planet's London office and produced by: **Commissioning Editor** Paula Hardy **Coordinating Editor** Evan Jones **Coordinating Cartographer** Jacqueline Nguyen **Coordinating Layout Designer** Katherine Marsh **Managing Editor** Brigitte Ellemor **Managing Cartographers** David Connolly, Mark Griffiths **Managing Layout Designers** Laura Jane, Celia Wood **Assisting Editors** Simone Egger, Martine Power **Assisting Cartographer** Joanne Luke **Cover Designer** Tamsin Wilson **Project Manager** Rachel Imeson **Language Content Coordinator** Quentin Frayne **Thanks to** John Mazzocchi, Adam Bextream, Lisa Knights

ISBN 978 1 74104 717 2

Printed by Hang Tai Printing Company, China.

HOW TO USE THIS BOOK
Colour-Coding & Maps

Colour-coding is used for symbols on maps and in the text that they relate to (eg all eating venues on the maps and in the text are given a green knife and fork symbol). Each neighbourhood also gets its own colour, and this is used down the edge of the page and throughout that neighbourhood section.

Shaded yellow areas on the maps denote 'areas of interest' — for their historical significance, their attractive architecture or their great bars and restaurants. We encourage you to head to these areas and just start exploring!

Prices

Multiple prices listed with reviews (eg €10/5 or €10/5/20) indicate adult/child, adult/concession or adult/child/family.

Send us your feedback We love to hear from readers — your comments help make our books better. We read every word you send us, and we always guarantee that your feedback goes straight to the appropriate authors. The most useful submissions are rewarded with a free book. To send us your updates and find out about Lonely Planet events, newsletters and travel news visit our award-winning website: **lonelyplanet.com/contact**.

Note: We may edit, reproduce and incorporate your comments in Lonely Planet products such as guidebooks, websites and digital products, so let us know if you don't want your comments reproduced or your name acknowledged. For a copy of our privacy policy visit **lonelyplanet.com/privacy**.

ROBERT LANDON

Ten minutes into his maiden voyage to Florence, Robert was pick-pocketed in a shadowy nave of Santa Maria Novella. Despite the band of child-thieves, he's returned to the city obsessively for two decades, including many too-brief visits, a particularly satisfying sojourn in the Oltrarno, a lost weekend in Fiesole, and a long, hot summer funded with misappropriated student loans. Robert studied Italian at Stanford University, and has also lived a half a year in Rome. Currently based in Rio de Janeiro and San Francisco, he writes about travel, arts and business for a range of publications, from the *Los Angeles Times* to CNET.com, and has written several other Lonely Planet titles.

ROBERT'S THANKS

Grazie mille to Alberto Giovannini and the Campucci gang (for insights and hospitality); Marco Mazzoni (good behaviour); Mom (company, especially shared meals); Neri Torrigiani (tripe sandwich); Nicola Williams (tips, text); Paula Hardy (enthusiasm, incisiveness); Carlos Ponce (cats, plants); and Thiago Fico (increasingly declarative correspondence on the road and kind attention at write-up).

THE PHOTOGRAPHER
GIORGIO COSULICH

Giorgio Cosulich works as a freelance photographer and is based in Rome. His career in photography, which began in 1995, has taken him around the world including to many conflict zones. Giorgio's photos have appeared in many major newspapers and magazines including the *New York Times*, *Stern* and *Time*.

Cover photograph Fountain in Piazza Frescobaldi, near Ponte Santa Trinita in Florence, Italy, Stefano Amantini/ Corbis. **Internal photographs** p47, 68, 79, 98, 127, 132 by Robert Landon; p10 Stefano Amantini/4Corners Images; p27 Kaos03/SIME/4Corners Images; p29 Stefano Amantini/4Corners Images. All other photographs by Lonely Planet Images, and by Giorgio Cosulich except p13, 156 Martin Moos; p14 Greg Elms; p17, 106, 145 Diana Mayfield; p24, 67, 104, 150, 155 Juliet Coombe; p26, 62, 65, 89, 92, 159 Martin Hughes; p44 Olivier Cirendini; p139 Philip & Karen Smith; p143 Wayne Walton; p146 Jon Davison; p148 John Hay; p149 John Elk III; p162 Richard Cummins; p165 Andrew Peacock; p166 Juliet Coombe. All images are copyright of the photographers unless otherwise indicated. Many of the images in this guide are available for licensing from **Lonely Planet Images**: www.lonelyplanetimages.com.

The Piazza della Signoria (p49) is best appreciated either before or after the crowds have dispersed

CONTENTS

THIS IS FLORENCE

For the discerning traveller, Florence begs a question: Is this a living city or a glorified museum? The answer is 'yes' on both counts.

According to Unesco, Florence (Firenze in Italian) contains 'the greatest concentration of universally renowned works of art in the world'. They issue no disclaimers. Of course, greatest hits such as *David* and *The Birth of Venus* also attract seemingly the world's greatest concentration of tourists. You must suffer them, wade through them, queue with them to see the most iconic of the Michelangelos, Masaccios and Botticellis.

But just blocks off the tourist itineraries, Florence manages to conduct plenty of 21st-century business. It remains an industrious regional capital and a fierce mini-capital of fashion from where Milan buys its leathers and fabrics. It's both a deep well of leftist agitation and a rich font of haute-bourgeois finery. And after checking their email, Oltrarno artisans go back to banging, firing and polishing, as they have since medieval times.

Indeed, art and commerce – like locals and tourists, past and present – are forced into close contact on the city's narrow streets, rubbing one another raw yet leading to fruitful syntheses. In this sense, Florence remains unchanged since the days when, above the great gulf of the Duomo's medieval transept, cloth merchants hired Brunelleschi to raise his primal Renaissance dome.

Sitting on an unnavigable river in a valley of middling agricultural productivity, the city has been forced to prosper on ingenuity: fine craftsmanship, creative banking practices, slick diplomacy. But its growth has always run up against natural limits. Rome and Milan could tear themselves down and rebuild many times, whereas central Florence looks much as it did in 1550, with its stone towers and red-tiled domes, cypress-lined gardens and frescoed monasteries, lazy, dun-coloured river and layered vistas past green hills to smoky blue peaks. The effect is rather like a Renaissance painting, which of course makes perfect sense when you think about it.

Top Left The 15th-century political carousel has been replaced by a more enjoyable one as seen in the Piazza della Repubblica (p49) **Bottom Left** A sample of Masaccio's wonderful frescoes inside Cappella Brancacci (p123)

>HIGHLIGHTS

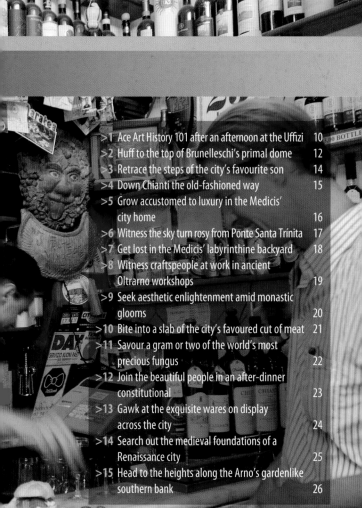

Join the action inside I Fratellini's popular food and wine stall (p54)

>1 GALLERIA DEGLI UFFIZI

ACE ART HISTORY 101 AFTER AN AFTERNOON AT THE UFFIZI

One of the cleverest buildings of the Renaissance, Giorgio Vasari's U-shaped, light-flooded Palazzo degli Uffizi (p45) was built to house the offices from which the Medici could run their growing dukedom. These days the palazzo contains that family's greatest legacy – what is, quite simply, the world's finest collection of Renaissance art. Sheer numbers begin to tell the story: more than 1500 works distributed across 50 rooms.

However, it is the sustained quality of the collection that makes it extraordinary. The sweeping narrative begins with the forerunners of the Renaissance such as Giotto, Cimabue and Simone Martini's shimmering *Annunciazione,* and culminates with its inheritors such as Titian and Caravaggio.

Even so, pride of place goes to Florence's home-grown maestros. Botticelli garners most gasps with his iconic *Birth of Venus* and *Spring* – both arrestingly fresh no matter how many reproductions you've seen. Tuscan-born Leonardo da Vinci makes his appearance with the exquisite *Annunciazione,* as does Michelangelo with a distinctly muscular Holy Family in his *Tondo Doni*. With a collection of this calibre, names such as Rafael, Rubens and Rembrandt are practically also-rans.

The museum's curators help visitors navigate this dizzying array by following a more or less strict chronological order, starting with the Tuscan masters of the 12th to 14th century, then moving in order through the Renaissance pioneers, High Renaissance and mannerism, and baroque and neoclassical periods. If you want to take it all in, one visit is not enough. Better to pick a period, a set of works, or a particular artist to concentrate your viewing, and then gather ideas for a return visit.

The staff of the Uffizi know they have a good thing, and some say this means they've felt no need to innovate. Crowds are too large, lines are too long though avoidable (p41), and many of the rooms are regrettably cramped. However, a (gasp!) minimalist Japanese-designed exit facade and promise of larger, more modern exhibition rooms are firmly on the docket (p45).

If you have the brain cells left, the palazzo itself is worth a little attention. Its blessedly wide corridors, capped by delightful ceiling frescoes, give a sense of airiness that many other galleries lack, plus the passage facing the Arno proffers wonderful views up to San Miniato al Monte (p26). The cafe provides equally stunning views across Piazza della Signoria. Finally, the secret Corridoio Vasariano (p48), which starts in the bowels of the Uffizi, takes the privileged few across the Ponte Vecchio and all the way to Palazzo Pitti, without ever stepping outside. For more on the Uffizi, see p45.

> 2 THE DUOMO

HUFF TO THE TOP OF BRUNELLESCHI'S PRIMAL DOME

Brunelleschi's red-tiled dazzler of a dome represents two feats of genius. First there's the fact that he was able to build it at all. No one had tried such a feat since Roman times. Nearly 115m high and 42m wide, it remains, nearly six centuries after its completion in 1436, the largest masonry dome in the world.

Then of course there's the sheer loveliness of his creation, with its eight marble ribs, gold-appointed lantern and four million bricks that seemingly float above the city's rooftops. More pointed than a perfect dome, it both reaches towards heaven and remains firmly planted in the heart of the city's worldly affairs.

Yes, it's worth the long huff up the 463 increasingly narrow steps to the top. The vistas are staggering. The narrative begins with the narrow walkway that surrounds the inner base of the dome. Look up for a close-up of Vasari's *Last Judgment* that fills the dome's interior. Its celestial hosts and hellish torments are depicted in a muscular style influenced by Michelangelo's Sistine Chapel. Then look down and, besides a nice case of vertigo, you get a bird's-eye view of the vast cathedral interior below, including the beguiling geometry of its marble pavements.

Next you get to see up close exactly how Brunelleschi achieved his miracle, because the next set of steps actually sits in between two separate domes, one inside the other. This doubling enabled one dome to hold up the other as construction continued across the vast gulf. The two domes grow closer and closer as you climb, until a trap door opens up onto the final goal of your journey: heavenly 360-degree vistas of Florence, Fiesole and the Apennines.

And don't forget that the Duomo encompasses far more than a dome. The cathedral complex also includes Giotto's flowerlike *campanile* (bell tower; p44) and the Museo dell'Opera del Duomo (p45), with statues by Donatello and Michelangelo as well as the machines Brunelleschi invented from scratch to build his dome. Finally, behind Ghiberti's golden doors (the originals are actually in the Museo dell'Opera del Duomo), the womblike Battistero (Baptistery) reveals its jewel-like Romanesque mosaics. Long considered

a Roman temple because of its classical motifs, it's actually an 11th-century creation built just as Florence began to grow into the prospering city that would, a few centuries on, possess the will and means to build the world's largest dome. See also p44.

>3 MICHELANGELO
RETRACE THE STEPS OF THE CITY'S FAVOURITE SON

At once the fullest flower of the Renaissance and the first to tran-
scend its limits, the works of Michelangelo writhe with what his
biographer Giorgio Vasari called *terribilità:* terrifying grandeur. Witness his *David,* whose sinewy form bespeaks balance and repose at a
distance, but turns menacing when you meet his fierce eyes.

Michelangelo left his fellow Florentines a priceless, if widely dispersed, legacy. For his earliest works, head to Museo Casa Buonarroti
(p97), the aristocratic home paid for with papal commissions. Down
the street, the Museo del Bargello (p97) holds a drunken *Bacchus* and
bust of Brutus. The Uffizi boasts the genre-busting *Tondo Rondi* (p45),
his only known panel painting. The Museo dell'Opera del Duomo
(p45) gives pride of place to a heart-wrenching *Pietá*. And his addi-
tions to San Lorenzo (p73) make architectural historians swoon.

However, it's *David,* housed in the purpose-built Galleria
dell'Accademia (p87), who still brings in the biggest crowds. The
replica in Piazza della Signoria may be true to the original, but it lacks
that *terribilità* infused by the master's chisel.

>4 ENOTECHE

DOWN CHIANTI THE OLD-FASHIONED WAY

Ranging from holes in the wall to Renaissance palazzi, *enoteche* (wine bars) serve a vital function in Florentine life. The opening hours say it all. By 9am, corks are popping to ease the morning commute. Not coincidentally, the city's most celebrated restaurant, Enoteca Pinchiorri (p102), only opened its kitchen to pique tipplers' palates.

To accompany the wine, most *enoteche* serve small salty bits of food – *panini* (small sandwiches), *crostini* (toast with savoury topping) and hunks of meat and cheese – and don't even offer seating. The idea is to swig, not savour. Casa del Vino (p82) is an elegant example of the rustic school, with its carved wood cabinetry and short list of fine Tuscan pourings.

However, a new generation is updating the ancient tradition. Le Volpi e l'Uva (p118) offers an estimable pairing of wines and cheeses, plus sleek tables at which to imbibe. For those who prefer a full meal plus aristocratic digs, the Antinori family has opened up a portion of their 15th-century palazzo (p67) to well-heeled commoners who prefer the presence of linen tablecloths along with top-flight Chianti.

HIGHLIGHTS

>5 PALAZZO PITTI
GROW ACCUSTOMED TO LUXURY IN THE MEDICIS' CITY HOME

When the Medicis outgrew the Palazzo Vecchio in the 1540s, they settled on a 15th-century palazzo belonging to the Pitti, a rival banking family fallen on hard times. Of course the Medici expanded their new home enormously, and today the beautifully forbidding palace, with its rough-cut stone facade, sits like an aging soldier-king guarding Florence's southern flank.

These days, the palazzo (see also p114) has been divided into no less than six museums, including the apartments of Italy's 19th-century kings, a museum of 19th- and 20th-century Florentine art, and another devoted to Tuscan fashions. Out back, a graceful courtyard, designed by Bartolommeo Ammanati in the 1560s, links the fortresslike palazzo with the green delights of the Boboli gardens.

However, the Pitti's greatest treasures lie in the Galleria Palatina. In 28 rooms, damask-covered walls are hung thick with Renaissance paintings, often hung three-high or four-high. Unlike the Uffizi, quality varies, but there's no shortage of masterworks, including Raphael's *La Donna Velata* and Caravaggio's *Sleeping Cupid*.

>6 SUNSET ON THE ARNO

WITNESS THE SKY TURN ROSY FROM PONTE SANTA TRÍNITA

Florence's humid climate has at least one thing to recommend it. As the sun drops towards the west, the dense air is known to turn shades ranging from cupid pinks to infernal reds and oranges.

To watch the show in its Technicolor glory, head to Ponte Santa Trínita (p63). It attracts smaller crowds than neighbouring Ponte Vecchio and offers unbroken views west down the Arno. If the scene is not sweet enough for you, add a scoop of gelato from the excellent Gelateria Santa Trínita (p133), which sits just south of the bridge.

As the natural light wanes, look back east towards the Ponte Vecchio as lights from its ancient goldsmith shops shimmer on the darkening river.

>7 BOBOLI GARDENS

GET LOST IN THE MEDICIS' LABYRINTHINE BACKYARD

The Giardino di Boboli (p112) seems to gather in a single expanse all the greenery that has been squeezed out of stone-heavy central Florence. Largely a 16th-century creation, its artificial grottos and Roman statuary, geometric axes and hidden glades were originally destined for the private delight of the Medici. Leading mannerist artists had their hand in the garden's design, including Buontalenti and Ammanati.

Today the Boboli admits literally millions of visitors annually, though fortunately at nearly 45 hectares, there's room for relatively secluded rambling. To escape the crowds, head down the impressive, cypress-lined alley with its shady byways to Isolotto, an ornamental pond whose central island in spring is redolent with citrus blossoms.

>8 OLTRARNO ARTISANS

WITNESS CRAFTSPEOPLE AT WORK IN ANCIENT OLTRARNO WORKSHOPS

In our factory-made world, the clanging, sanding, sweat and sawdust of the Oltrarno's human-scale workshops is nothing less than heartening. Medieval guilds may be defunct, but many artisans still hand down their craft from generation to generation. And an admirable portion of valuable city-centre real estate is given over to the work of welders and goldsmiths, framers and bookbinders, shoemakers and seamstresses. Most are clustered around Piazza Santo Spirito, where they often come to share a bottle of wine when work is done and the weather is fair.

The results of their labours are remarkable, from Stefano Bemer's made-to-measure opera pumps (p130) to the trompe l'oeil marble mosaics of Pitti Mosaici (p129). So is the fact that in Florence, workshops also function as semipublic entertainment. Many artisans work behind plate-glass windows or in shops that double as workshops. The degree to which you are allowed into the inner sanctum will depend on the humour of individual artisans, the charm with which you approach them, and of course your readiness to buy.

>9 SANTA MARIA NOVELLA

SEEK AESTHETIC ENLIGHTENMENT AMID MONASTIC GLOOMS

A number of buildings vie for the title, but the Basilica di Santa Maria Novella (p59) gets our vote for birthplace of the Renaissance. Part of a rambling Dominican monastery, the church was completed in 1346 on austere, Gothic lines. However, its finishing flourishes form a revolutionary narrative told in paint and marble.

Credit for the pioneering facade, with its templelike pediment and graceful scrolls, goes to Leon Battista Alberti. Its harmonious proportions and classical motifs were completely novel at the time. Inside, Giotto's crucifix, with its dripping blood and nascent use of perspective, was ahead of the curve in the 1290s. However, it's a great leap to Masaccio's *Trínita* (1427). Widely considered the first painting of the Renaissance, it's set in a Roman temple that appears to recede deep into the church's wall.

Masaccio's innovations reach full flower in Ghirlandaio's Cappella Tornabuoni, the chapel that sits resplendently behind Brunelleschi's altar. The fresco cycle, completed in the 1480s, depicts Mary as a contemporary patrician Florentine whose wealth endowed the Renaissance itself.

>10 BISTECCA ALLA FIORENTINA
BITE INTO A SLAB OF THE CITY'S FAVOURED CUT OF MEAT

As thick and bloody as Florentine history and even more delightful to ingest, *bistecca alla fiorentina* (Florentine-style T-bone steak) is the crown jewel of Florentine cuisine.

Like much of Tuscan cooking, ingredients are few and preparation simple. The steak, in short, must speak for itself. To that end, it should be grilled over wood coals, preferably oak or olive – red-hot but not flaming. The only other ingredients – salt and pepper – come only after the cooking.

The real trick, though, is the cow. A true *bistecca* comes from the prized Chianina breed. The result: a great slab of pleasure, crusty outside and succulently crimson inside, with a T-bone that adds its own volume of flavour.

A couple of caveats for the carnivorous. Skip lunch or plan to share your *bistecca*. If it's less than 5cm thick and 1.2 kilos, you've been had. Many restaurants offer *bistecca* for €40 per kilo, but spend a little more (up to €60) at a high-end establishment to guarantee it's Chianina on your plate.

>11 TRUFFLE HUNT

SAVOUR A GRAM OR TWO OF THE WORLD'S MOST PRECIOUS FUNGUS

Ugly to behold, impossible to cultivate and possessing flavours that beggar description, *tartufo bianco* (white truffle) is the most precious ingredient of the Florentine kitchen.

Each autumn, the San Miniato hills, 30km west of Florence, yield hundreds of kilograms of the fungus, which grows symbiotically along the roots of oak, hazel, poplar and beech trees. Specially trained dogs sniff them out, and the happy hunter can sell the stuff for up to €1000 per kilogram.

Fortunately, a few grams can make an entire plate of pasta sing with earthy, nutty aromas. November is high season, when truffle-infused dishes appear on menus across the city. For bite-sized tastes at remarkably reasonable prices any time of the year, head to ultra-genteel Procacci (p56) or Olio & Convivium (p135, see photo).

>12 FARE IL GIRO

JOIN THE BEAUTIFUL PEOPLE IN AN AFTER-DINNER CONSTITUTIONAL

To maintain one's full citizenship in Florence, it's necessary to dress up, descend to the streets and devote an hour or so to *fare il giro* (literally, 'to do a turn'). Indeed, in a city where the highest virtues are aesthetic, to appear in one's finest is to assert one's very existence. The ideal time is early on a weekend evening, though any hour will do as long as you're sufficiently dapper and self-possessed.

Fare il giro usually involves a saunter through the closest piazza or two – or maybe the Piazza della Signoria, with requisite stops to gossip with neighbours. You're sure to cross one or two in this modest-sized city. Otherwise, satisfy yourself with private appraisals of shop windows, the weather, the state of dress of your fellows, and the galling scaffolding on some interminably delayed municipal project.

A cup of gelato makes an excellent accompaniment, though you must patronise your own *gelateria,* not the one everyone else has been praising to high heaven but that you know very well has started cutting corners.

>13 WINDOW DROOLING

GAWK AT THE EXQUISITE WARES ON DISPLAY ACROSS THE CITY

At least since weaver-monks set up shop here in the 12th century, Florence has lived on luxury. However, in the last decade or so, Gucci's hometown has refashioned itself into a shopper's paradise, with dozens of swank new shops on and around Via de' Tornabuoni. Across the Arno, Borgo San Jacopo harbours another bevy of luxury.

Clothing dominates, with shoes and handbags to make a person weep. All major labels are represented, but try seeking out local craftspeople such as Angela Caputi (p126) and Quelle Tre (p129), who offer one-of-a-kind fits. And either come armed with high credit limits, or join the rest of us, press your nose up to the glass, and salivate freely.

>14 MEDIEVAL FLORENCE

SEARCH OUT THE MEDIEVAL FOUNDATIONS OF A RENAISSANCE CITY

While the crowds come seeking the Renaissance, Florence is ironically among Europe's best-preserved medieval cities. Thank Florentines for their natural frugality, which prevented the destruction of perfectly good medieval keeps. And when the city lost its monopolies on banking and cloth markets in the 16th and 17th centuries, there was that much less left for renovations.

Today, the city centre is dense with both forbidding stone towers and the elegant homes of Middle Ages moguls such as the Palazzo Davanzati (p46). The naves of Santa Croce (p96) and Santa Maria Novella (p59) are distinctly Gothic, as is the jewel-like Orsanmichele (p46; see photo), with its elaborately carved windows and bejewelled tabernacle. And the crenulated towers of the Museo del Bargello (p97) and Palazzo Vecchio (p48) are the highest achievements of a burgeoning medieval city-state.

Not old enough for you? Take note of the gridlike streets between the Duomo and the Palazzo Vecchio, which still follow the pattern laid out by Julius Caesar's army when they set up camp here about 59 BC.

HIGHLIGHTS

>15 UP TO SAN MINIATO

HEAD TO THE HEIGHTS ALONG THE ARNO'S GARDENLIKE SOUTHERN BANK

From the hills along the Arno's south bank, an unlikely swathe of Tuscan countryside, complete with flowering orchards, olive groves and even a rustic church, spills down almost to the city centre. Most of the land is walled off to the public, but a series of winding lanes and stone footpaths looks out over this privileged terrain.

However, these charms are only part of the story. Your ascent leads to San Miniato al Monte (p109), an 11th-century Romanesque church that is at once Florence's oldest and most delightful with its green-and-white facade and arresting marble floors. When you arrive at the church doors, look back and see Florence laid out before you, its red roofs crowned and ordered by Brunelleschi's serene dome.

For an even longer ramble (p119), a new ticketing system provides an almost unbroken greenway that encompasses the sprawling Giardino di Boboli (p112), the grassy prospects of Forte di Belvedere (p109), and perfectly tended Giardino di Bardini (p109) with its own, more intimate views onto the city's rooftops.

>FLORENCE DIARY

Even in apostate Florence, much of the social calendar revolves around the Church, beginning with pre-Lenten Carnivale celebrations (February to March) then Easter, the Festa di San Giovanni (June) and Christmas. May is the busiest month for secular culture, with the world-renowned Maggio Musicale Fiorentino music festival, the alternative Fabbrica Europa arts festival and the elegant Artigianato e Palazzo arts and crafts festival. In the summer, Estate Fiesolana brings live performances to Fiesole's Roman amphitheatre and a number of outdoor cinemas around the city. In July and August activity slows significantly.

Period costumes come out in force during the Scoppio del Carro (Explosion of the Cart; p28)

FEBRUARY & MARCH

Carnivale

A smattering of parties marks Florence's pre-Lenten season, though the real party, including an impressive parade, takes place in the seaside town of Viareggio, about 30km northwest of Pisa.

MARCH & APRIL

Scoppio del Carro

On Easter Sunday a costumed entourage escorts a wooden cart loaded with fireworks through the streets of Florence, and the cart is then ritually exploded in the Piazza del Duomo. Just outside Florence, Grassina's re-creation of the Passion of Christ (www.rievstoricagrassina.it) on Good Friday is impressive with its period costumes and a cast of hundreds.

MAY

Maggio Musicale Fiorentino

www.maggiofiorentino.com, in Italian
Led by Zubin Mehta, this month-long festival attracts some of the leading lights from the world of classical music, dance and theatre to Florence's Teatro Communale.

Fabbrica Europa

www.ffeac.org
For three weeks in May contemporary and avant-garde artists and performers display their talents in the recently refurbished Stazione Leopolda, a former train station at the western edge of this historical centre.

Artigianato e Palazzo

www.artigianatoepalazzo.it, in Italian
During a three-day weekend in the middle of May, master artisans from around Tuscany gather in the elegant gardens of the Palazzo Corsini offering a rare opportunity to see these privately held Renaissance-style gardens.

SUMMER-LONG EVENTS
Cinema Under the Stars

From June to August, outdoor cinemas pop up around the city, with programs ranging from Pasolini to *Die Hard*. Locations tend to change yearly. Tourist offices offer current listings and locations. One caveat: films are usually dubbed into Italian, and mosquitoes can be fierce.

Estate Fiesolana

www.estatefiesolana.it
From June to September, Fiesole (p140) hosts classical, jazz and world music concerts in its Roman-era amphitheatre, with the Tuscan countryside as its backdrop. There are related events throughout the town's churches and museums.

Double the fun: participants at the Calcio Storico (p30) during the Festa di San Giovanni (p30)

JUNE

Calcio Storico

www.calciostorico.it

After cancellation for excessive violence in 2007, Florence's spectacular, free-for-all version of football resumed in 2008. By tradition, two preliminary matches occur at the beginning of June, with the final in Piazza Santa Croce during the Festa di San Giovanni on 24 June. The game dates at least to Renaissance times, with origins said to reach back to ancient Rome.

Festa di San Giovanni

Besides the final Calcio Storico match in Santa Croce, Florentines celebrate their patron saint on 24 June with a grand religious procession and impressive fireworks display.

JULY & AUGUST

Il Palio

www.ilpalio.org

In one of Italy's most impressive displays of pageantry, the neighbourhoods of Siena (p146) dressed in colourful, historical costumes, compete in a pair of horse races (2 July, 15 August) that take place in the city's splendid Piazza del Campo.

DECEMBER

Nativity Scenes

The Christmas season brings Nativity scenes throughout Florence. Traditionally, the most elaborate are those in the Duomo, San Lorenzo and Santa Croce.

Approaching the Basilica di Santa Croce (p96) from its piazza

ITINERARIES

A small city with virtually all its sights clustered in just a few square kilometres, Florence is a place that you can get to know well, if not intimately, in a relatively short time. Still, the combination of crowds and staggering number of options make planning a big plus.

DAY ONE

Even those returning to Florence should consider joining the crowds plying their way from the Galleria dell'Accademia (p87) to the Duomo (p44), onto Piazza Signoria and the Uffizi (p45), then over Ponte Vecchio (p50) to the Giardino di Boboli (p112). Set on seeing Michelangelo's *David* and/or the Uffizi? Book in advance (see p41) or head to a ticket outlet first thing. To climb the Duomo, try after 4pm, after tour buses head off. Need a break? Escape into a hidden nook of the Boboli with a picnic lunch. For dinner try a classic Tuscan meal in the Oltrarno (p130).

DAY TWO

Start out with a cappuccino and a croissant at your neighbourhood cafe. If you've missed any big sights on Day One, now's the time. Then head for one of the great monastic churches, such as Santa Maria Novella (p59), Santa Croce (p96) or San Marco (p89). For lunch, try one of the city's excellent pizzerias, such as Il Pizzaiuolo (p102) or I Tarocchi (p117). In the afternoon, unwind and stretch your legs with a ramble up to San Miniato al Monte (p109). For a light dinner, indulge in another Florentine tradition – *aperitivi* buffet (see the boxed text, p56).

DAY THREE

With the top sights under your belt, consider the Museo del Bargello (p97) and/or labyrinthine Palazzo Vecchio (p48). Then lunch at one of the city's hearty sandwich stops such as I Fratellini (p54) or Antico Noè (p101). In the afternoon, head to one of the monastic churches you missed on Day Two. If you fancy the outdoors instead, consider a sunset ramble in Fiesole (p140). Back in town, unwind with a glass of Chianti at an *enoteca* (wine bar; p15) followed by a juicy *bistecca alla fiorentina* (T-bone steak; p21).

Top left The rustic interior of the Caffè degli Artigiani (p131) **Bottom left** The Museo di San Marco (p89) celebrates the works of its most famous past resident, artist Fra Angelico

RAINY DAY

In Florence, rain is no damper. Any of the churches and museums are fair game. The smart shops along Via de' Tornabuoni and Borgo San Jacopo also provide free shelter. Cafes such as classic Gilli (p55) and bohemian Libreria Café de la Cité (p137) make great refuges until the end of the downpour.

FAR FROM THE MADDING CROWD

The Museo del Bargello (p97), San Marco (p89) and San Lorenzo (p73) are top-flight sights that generally attract lighter crowds. Even better are the one-off masterpieces such as those in Cenacolo di Sant'Apollonia (p78), Chiostro dello Scalzo (p86) and Basilica di Santa Trínita (p59). The side streets of the Oltrarno are charming and uncrowded, as is the walk up to San Miniato al Monte (p26).

Explore luxe boutiques along Borgo San Jacopo (Map pp124-5), one of Florence's premier shopping streets

FORWARD PLANNING

Accommodation in Florence fills quickly, especially from April to June and September to October. Definitely book ahead. If possible, avoid visiting on holiday weekends, especially around Easter, 1 May and 15 August. If you want a seat at one of the top restaurants such as Enoteca Pinchiorri (p102) or Ristorante Cibrèo (p103), make reservations up to one month ahead if possible. And to ensure seeing the Uffizi or *David*, reserve your spot several weeks in advance if possible (see the boxed text, p41).

FOR FREE

In a city that lives on tourism, little in Florence is free. Even some churches are ticketed. San Miniato is a fine exception, as is the beautiful walk up to it (p26). Or you can take a city bus to Fiesole (p140) for free walks and million-dollar views. Some of the most spectacular in situ art is also free (p162). And a bottle of wine and a beautiful piazza make a complete evening.

>NEIGHBOURHOODS

Time out to talk, to plan, to observe or just have a well-earned rest at the Piazza della Signoria (p49)

NEIGHBOURHOODS

The falling fortunes of Florence in the 1500s brought good luck for today's traveller. As the city's economy sputtered out, Florence lacked the means to expand or even remodel, so that the historic core looks much as it did to Michelangelo. All its major sights lie within the tight ring once formed by its medieval walls.

The gridlike streets between the Duomo and Piazza della Signoria date to Roman times and remain Florence's political and cultural heart. Here you also find the lion's share of sights, from the Uffizi to Brunelleschi's dome.

The rest of the city's big-ticket items are distributed evenly around the ring of neighbourhoods, each anchored by its namesake monastery, that radiate out from this core. West of the centre, Santa Maria Novella is the city's transport hub (including train and bus stations) and home to its most elegant boutiques and cafes.

Heading clockwise, you reach San Lorenzo. Once the Medicis' stomping ground, it's now a workaday district of busy commercial streets. However, in their midst lies the extraordinary San Lorenzo complex. San Lorenzo blends seamlessly into San Marco, whose streets are equally commercial but more charming. To give an idea of scale, its two must-sees – Museo di San Marco and Galleria dell'Accademia – are just a few minutes' walk from the Duomo.

Continuing around, you reach Santa Croce. Its namesake basilica is, like Santa Maria Novella's, a lesson in art history. Santa Croce is also home to the city's top restaurants and liveliest bars.

Moving across the Arno, you reach the city's only stretch of green, including the Boboli gardens and the hillside orchards that surround it. Meanwhile, some of the city's best nightlife lurks down along the riverbanks.

Finally, you reach the Oltrarno district. Its narrow streets and placid squares harbour artisans and their swish shops, excellent and varied dining, and a buzzing, student-driven nightlife.

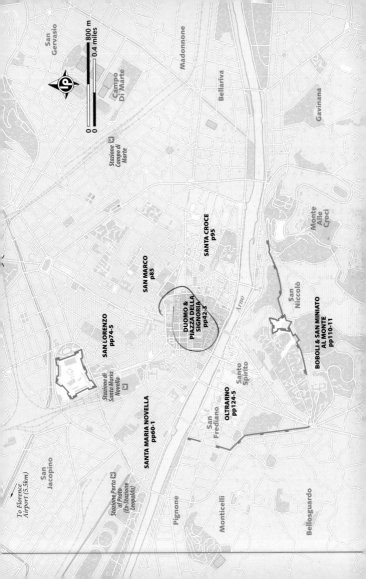

>DUOMO & PIAZZA DELLA SIGNORIA

Both the springboard for the Renaissance and the busy heart of modern Florence, the tight grid of streets between the Duomo and Piazza della Signoria packs a gigantic historical and artistic wallop in just a few hectares. Dotted with forbidding medieval towers predating Dante, the streets themselves are actually far older, still preserving the plans of the original Roman settlement. Piazza della Signoria, the city's natural amphitheatre, serves as its civic and social headquarters, while Brunelleschi's red dome stands sentinel over the scene. And did we mention the Uffizi? Of course this great density of sights means many of the narrow streets are often choked with tourists. After visiting the sights by day, return in the evening when the clamouring subsides and you can gape at both the remarkable whole and the soft glow of its individual parts.

DUOMO & PIAZZA DELLA SIGNORIA

Please see over for map

CUT THE QUEUE

During summer as well as holiday weekends, the queues at choice Florentine museums – notably the Uffizi and Accademia – can involve hot, sticky, half-day waits. The good news is, a dependable new booking system can slash your waiting time to zero (or, in the case of the Uffizi at peak times, up to one hour).

For a fee of €4 you can reserve tickets online at all of the 13 *musei statali* (state museums), including the Uffizi Gallery, Galleria dell'Accademia (where *David* lives), Palazzo Pitti, Museo del Bargello, Museo Archeologico and the Medici chapels (Cappelle Medicee). To get into the Uffizi or Accademia in high season, make reservations at least six weeks in advance. Remember that when you do make the reservation you must pick a time as well as a day.

If you're already in Florence, head to the ticket office of any of the above museums to make your reservation. There is also an outlet on Via de' Calzaiuoli in the rear of Orsanmichele. Often you can find times not available on the internet – though don't count on that at peak times.

On the day of your visit, signs shepherd prebooked ticket holders to a different entrance; in summer you might well have to queue twice – first to pay for/collect your ticket then again to actually get into the museum.

Still out of luck? Try joining a tour group. Most hotels and B&Bs can book tours.

◉ SEE

◉ BADIA FIORENTINA
Via Dante Alighieri; ⌚ **4.30-6.30pm Mon**
Founded in 979 by the Countess Matilda of Tuscany, the woman who also granted the city its liberty upon her death, the Badia Fiorentina (Florentine Abbey) is among the city's oldest institutions built just as Florence emerged from the Dark Ages. Except for the Romanesque *campanile* (bell tower), today's church is largely a Renaissance construct, with a splendid coffered ceiling and Filippino Lippi's *Apparition of the Virgin to St Bernard* to your left as you enter through the small cloister. It is here that Dante (see p52) watched Beatrice at her prayers in the 1270s. The church is only open to visitors two hours a week. Otherwise it is reserved for prayer and meditation only.

◉ BATTISTERO
☎ **055 230 28 85; www.duomofirenze .com; €3; Piazza del Duomo;** ⌚ **noon-7pm Mon-Sat, 8.30am-2pm Sun, 8.30am-2pm 1st Sat of month**
The 11th-century **Baptistery** is one of Florence's oldest buildings – and most extraordinary. The three doorways into the octagonal, Romanesque structure tell the story of humanity's redemption, including a revolutionary pair by sculptor Lorenzo Ghiberti that, in the early

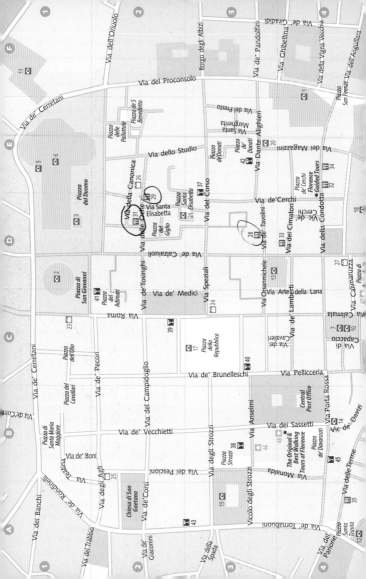

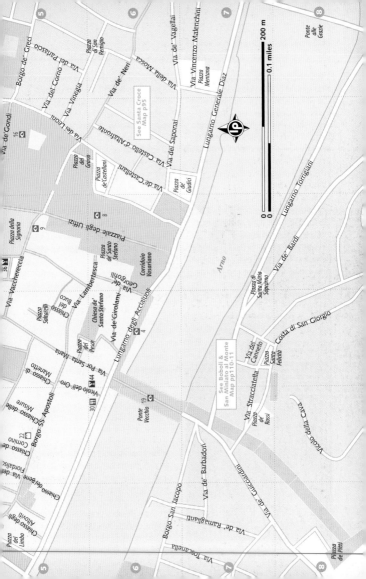

1400s, helped usher in a new age that would become known as the Renaissance (the originals are in Museo dell'Opera del Duomo, opposite). The womblike interior dazzles with its opulent, Byzantine-style mosaics, including a gruesome image of Satan devouring sinners, which is said to have inspired Dante's *Inferno*.

CAMPANILE
☎ 055 230 28 85; www.duomofirenze.com; €6; Piazza del Duomo; ⏱ 8.30am-7.30pm

Begun in 1334 by Giotto, the cathedral's soaring **bell tower** rises nearly as high as the cathedral's dome. Its elaborate Gothic facade, includ-

ing 16 life-size statues, represents a Who's Who of 14th-century art, including Giotto Andrea Pisano, Donatello and Luca Della Robbia (the originals are in Museo dell'Opera del Duomo, opposite). Climb its 414 steps for nearly the same superb city view as Brunelleschi's dome without the snaking lines.

DUOMO
☎ 055 230 28 85; www.duomofirenze.com; Piazza del Duomo; ⏱ 10am-5pm Mon-Wed & Fri, 10am-3.30pm Thu, 10am-4.45pm Sat, 1.30-4.45pm Sun, 1st Sat of month 10am-3.30pm

Begun in 1296 by Sienese architect Arnolfo di Cambio, the world's fourth-largest cathedral took almost 150 years to complete. Behind the Gothic welter of its white, green and red marble facade (actually a 19th-century re-creation), the interior of the city's **cathedral** is surprisingly Spartan, as most of its treasures have been moved to the adjacent **Museo dell'Opera del Duomo** (opposite). However, the vast and soaring space still houses masterpieces such as Uccello's portrait of Sir John Hawkwood and Michelino's fresco *Dante e I Suoi Mondi* (Dante and His Worlds). The gorgeously geometric marble paving is best appreciated when climbing up to Brunelleschi's **cupola del duomo** (cathedral dome, p12). A stairway near the main entrance of the

The Duomo as seen from Giotto's Campanile

cathedral leads down to the **crypt** (admission €3; ⏰ 10am-5pm Mon-Fri, 10am-4.45pm Sat), where archaeologists have uncovered the foundations of the 5th-century church that once occupied this site, as well as even older Roman artefacts.

☒ GALLERIA DELGI UFFIZI

☎ 055 238 86 51; www.polomuseale .firenze.it; €6.50; Piazzale degli Uffizi 6; ⏰ 8.15am-6.50pm Tue-Sun

Reason enough to come to Florence, this fabled museum (see also p10) contains quite simply the world's finest collection of Renaissance art, including both 12th- to 14th-century forebears and 16th- and 17th-century inheritors. Its 50-plus rooms are crammed with more than 1500 works, nearly all of them masterpieces. Part of the museum's mystique is the difficulties it presents: long lines, crowded galleries, a daunting combination of quantity and quality. There are two tricks to enjoying your experience: prebook tickets (p41) and concentrate on select artists or periods. While signage is less than satisfying, the museum is laid out chronologically, and largely over a single floor. For a mental-health break, head to the **roof-top cafe** (only accessible once you're in), which serves up fresh air, light snacks and wonderful views over Piazza della Signoria and beyond.

A 21ST CENTURY UFFIZI – POSSIBLE AS SOON AS THE 22ND CENTURY

The Uffizi has been threatening to expand its exhibition space for generations. A decade of debate has raged over a portico in contemporary style over its main exit. And cranes have graced its graceful courtyard for several years. At the time of writing, none of these projects had come to full fruition, and tourist officials were unwilling to make any promises. Officials say that the portico should be completed by 2011. Don't hold your breath.

☒ MUSEO DELL'OPERA DEL DUOMO

☎ 055 230 28 85; www.duomofirenze .com; €6; Piazza del Duomo 9; ⏰ 9am-7.30pm Mon-Sat, 9am-1.40pm Sun

Light, airy and surprisingly overlooked by the crowds, the **Cathedral Museum** behind the cathedral safeguards works that once adorned the Duomo, Battistero (Baptistery) and *campanile*. The museum begins with a history of the Duomo told in the best English-language signage in Florence. Under the glass-topped courtyard you'll find the original version of Ghiberti's awe-inspiring masterpiece – the *Porta del Paradiso* (Doors of Paradise). Designed for the Battistero, the doors took 27 painstaking years to complete and are considered a seminal work of the early

Renaissance for their naturalism and innovative use of perspective. Other masterworks in the museum include Michelangelo's *Pietà*, a work he intended for his own tomb, and Donatello's wooden representation of a gaunt and desolate *Mary Magdalene*. Upstairs, you can also see the original machines Brunelleschi designed to build his revolutionary dome (p12).

◉ ORSANMICHELE

☎ 055 284 944; Via Arte della Lana; 🕑 10am-5pm Tue-Sun

This odd jewel of a building started out as a grain market that was walled in during the 14th century to create a church, though the upper floors remained a working granary. This strange concoction is a reminder of how religious, commercial and civic life were intertwined in medieval Florence. With its lacelike stone window frames and gold and lapis lazuli tabernacle, it's a masterpiece of Italian Gothic. Outdoor niches are populated with masterworks of the early Renaissance with statues by the likes of Donatello, Ghiberti and Brunelleschi (most are copies as the originals have been moved to the Museo del Bargello, p97).

◉ PALAZZO DAVANZATI

☎ 055 27 76 461; www.polomuseale .firenze.it/davanzati; Via Porta Rossa 13;

🕑 8.15am-1.50pm, closed 2nd & 4th Sun, 1st, 3rd & 5th Mon of month

The scale and luxury of this 14th-century palazzo are a reminder of the medieval wealth that helped fund the coming Renaissance, from its monumental courtyard to the leaded glass that covers its rooftop kitchen. Around the courtyard, the maze of rooms contains a collection of period furnishing and utensils. There are free guided tours at 10am, 11am and noon most days.

◉ MERCATO NUOVO

Now trading only in second-rate souvenirs, this elegant *loggia* (roofed, open-air structure often on the side of a building) was built in the 16th century to shelter wool, silk and gold merchants under its classically inspired arches and columns. The adjacent **Fontana del Porcellino** (Piglet Fountain) stars a bronze boar (a 17th-century copy of the Greek marble original in the Uffizi) whose snout has been rubbed smooth by tourist hands. According to legend, a rub and a coin in the fountain guarantees your return to Florence.

◉ MUSEO FERRAGAMO

☎ 055 276 82 24; www.ferragamo.it; €5; Piazza Santa Trínita 5r; 🕑 10am-6pm Wed-Mon

In the basement of a fine medieval palace that also houses

Niccolò Salvestrini
Historian, tour leader, native Florentine

'Florence can feel like Renaissance Disney,' admits Nicco, who leads tours for groups often spending just a half-day here before being bussed to Rome or Venice. A common question: 'Where's the Louvre?' Still, the city's delicate beauty manages to make a strong impression, he says. **What provokes the most gasps?** A glance up narrow medieval streets toward a marbled slice of the Duomo, then suddenly arriving on the Piazza del Duomo to witness its totality. 'People seem to understand intuitively that Florence's beauty is unique – a rare flower with roots in centuries of refinement.' **Is Nicco still awed by the Glory of the Renaissance?** 'Not really. What animates me – besides the money, of course – are my clients, the enthusiasm they feel, the questions they ask when seeing it for the first time.' **Nicco's tip to beat the crowds:** Seek out art in situ (p162) such as Castagna's *Last Supper* in Sant'Apollonia (p78).

Ferragamo's flagship store, this quirky museum is mandatory for shoe fetishists – others may find the admission price exorbitant for what you get. Besides some of the Florentine designer's most lavish creations, you can see pumps made to order for the likes of Judy Garland and Marilyn Monroe.

◉ PALAZZO STROZZI

☎ 055 283 962; www.palazzostrozzi.org; Piazza Strozzi; ◷ times & prices vary

To outshine their Medici rivals, the Strozzi – another super-rich banking family – hired Giugliano de Sangallo to design their new city home in the 1480s. He constructed a massive but elegant fortress of rusticated stone that today hosts good temporary art exhibitions. The cafe on its colonnaded courtyard provides shelter from sun, rain and foot traffic – no ticket required.

◉ PALAZZO VECCHIO

☎ 055 276 82 24; adult/child 3-17yr/18-25yr €6/2/4.50; Piazza della Signoria; ◷ 9am-7pm Fri-Wed, 9am-2pm Thu

The seat of city government since the 1300s, this fortress-palace, with its soaring 94m-high Torre d'Arnolfo, is synonymous with Florence itself. Medici dukes turned the medieval building into a Renaissance palace in the 1500s, filling it with art and frescoes that still grace its labyrinth of rooms.

OPEN SECRET

If you have to move from one of your palatial city homes to another, why should you have to descend to the streets to do so? The Medicis saw no reason to, and in 1565 Cosimo I ordered court architect Giorgio Vasari to construct the **Corridoio Vasariano** (☎ 055 29 48 83; ◷ by guided tour on special request). The indoor promenade still provides an unbroken link between the Uffizi and the Palazzo Pitti all the way across the Arno.

Unfortunately, the corridor is still open only to a privileged few. Tours are available by special request but even if you can afford the fee – usually more than €100 per person – you have to know someone who knows someone even to get on the docket. There is talk of trying to make the system more 'transparent', though transparency has never been the Uffizi's strong point. Nor is expediting matters.

Too bad, because in addition to being fascinating in its own right, the corridor holds a fine collection of self-portraits by the likes of Bronzino, Bernini, Rubens and Rembrandt.

If you don't get lucky, at least you can trace its progress down the Arno, over Ponte Vecchio before disappearing into a medieval tower, then popping out to graze the front of Santa Felicità church before disappearing again into the mass of buildings that cluster next to the Pitti.

View the comings and goings of Florentine life in comfort at the Piazza della Signoria

Spring for the guided 'secret passage' (€2) tour, which takes you backstage into the Medicis' private digs. There are also good tours for children that include costumed re-enactments of Medici court life.

◎ PIAZZA DELLA REPUBBLICA
In the late 19th century, Florence decided to raze a dense maze of medieval dwellings to make way for the overblown Piazza della Repubblica. A triumphal arch reveals the vogue for all things Roman as a newly reunited nation tried to carve out its identity. Today the piazza is ringed by classic Victorian-era cafes such as Giubbe Rosse (p55) and Gilli (p55) as well as mostly high-end shops and hotels.

◎ PIAZZA DELLA SIGNORIA
The hub of city life since the Middle Ages, this irregular-shaped piazza is something of a Zelig, taking on completely different personalities depending on the hour, season and street by which you enter and exit. It's most beautiful after dark when tourist throngs have abated. The Palazzo Vecchio (opposite) dominates the square, dwarfing otherwise monumental works such as Ammannati's **Fontana di Nettuno** (Neptune Fountain) and Giambologna's equestrian statue of Cosimo I de' Medici. Note that the much-photographed *David* here is a copy. A plaque marks the spot where Savonarola (p86) was burnt at the stake. On its south

flank, the prospering 14th-century city-state built the **Loggia dei Lanzi**, to hold public ceremonies. Today, it serves as an open-air museum containing ancient and Renaissance sculpture, most of a violent nature, such as Giambologna's **Ratto delle Sabine** (Rape of the Sabine Women) and Cellini's **Perseus** brandishing the head of Medusa.

PONTE VECCHIO

Florence's oldest and most iconic bridge still defines the city's riverfront after nearly seven centuries. Once home to medieval butchers, its multistoried shops now proffer only gold and jewellery shops, due to a Medici edict dating to 1593. Unfortunately the bridge is hopelessly crowded from morning to night, and shops offer few bargains. Head to Ponte Santa Trínita, the next bridge to the west, to see the flowers spilling out of Ponte Vecchio's irregular tiers of windows as the Arno flows beneath the scene.

TORRE DELLA CASTAGNA
Via Dante Alighieri

Dating to the 1200s just as Florence was beginning to prosper as a textile and banking centre, Torre della Castagna is among the most impressive of the city's remaining medieval **towers**, of which there once were as many as 150. It's not open to visitors.

TORRE PAGLIAZZA
Piazza Santa Elisabetta

Regarded as the oldest building in Florence, this often-overlooked round stone **tower** probably dates to the 7th century and is of Byzantine origin. Today it has been incorporated into a hotel.

SHOP

ANGELA CAPUTI *Clothing*
☎ 055 292 993; www.angelacaputi.com; **Borgo Santissimi Apostoli 44/46**
Caputi's jewellery workshop is in the Oltrarno (p126), but here she also sells one-of-a-kind women's clothes gathered during her travels around the world, from avant-garde German hoodies to artisanal Japanese silks.

CALZOLERIA BOLOGNA
Shoes
☎ 055 290 545; www.calzoleriabologna.com; **Piazza di San Giovanni 13r**
Starring hometown shoemakers as well as Bolognese and foreign competitors, Florentines come here for eye-catching kicks at earth-bound (not bargain) prices. Even Converse comes with a twist.

LA RINASCENTE
Department Store
☎ 055 219 113; www.rinascente.it; **Piazza della Repubblica 1**; ⏰ 10am-9pm **Mon-Sat, 10.30am-8pm Sun**

Longer hours (including Sunday hours) plus the rooftop cafe with its winning views across Florence make this upscale if otherwise un-inspired department store worth a gander.

MICHELE NEGRI *Clothing*
☎ 055 212 781; Via degli Agli 3r
Spacious and minimalist, the flagship store of this casual-chic Florentine designer provides creative, rich-hued takes on classic men's and women's clothes, plus a cafe in the adjacent *loggia*.

PAPERBACK EXCHANGE *Books*
☎ 055 293 460; www.papex.it; Via delle Ocche 4r; 🕑 9am-7.30pm Mon-Fri, 10.30am-7.30pm Sat
Offering the city's widest selection of new and used English-language books, this bright little shop also hosts readings and other events.

PINEIDER *Stationery*
☎ 055 284 655; www.pineider.com; Piazza della Signoria 13/14r; 🕑 10am-7pm
Once purveyors to Napoleon, Pineider has been Florence's

A selection of wares from Pineider – definitely worth writing home about

NEIGHBOURHOODS

DUOMO & PIAZZA DELLA SIGNORIA

SERIOUS COMEDY

Both universal and quintessentially Florentine, the poetry of Dante Alighieri (c 1265–1321) is still considered Italy's finest. In fact, by writing with such power in the vernacular (rather than Latin) he helped shape the Italian language itself. When the peninsula was reunited in the 19th century, the Tuscan dialect became the young nation's new tongue, thanks largely to Dante's influence.

Born and raised in the streets between the Duomo and Piazza della Signoria, he fully participated in the city's political life – for which he paid a heavy price. Internecine feuds within his Guelf party forced him into exile, when he wrote much of his greatest work, *The Divine Comedy*. It traces his progress through Hell, Purgatory and Heaven where, unsurprisingly, he meets mostly deceased Florentines in various states of torment and ecstasy. His other great work, *La Vita Nuova* (New Life), is an extraordinary paean to Beatrice, his childhood love. It mixes poetry and prose with a curiously postmodern self-consciousness.

most exclusive stationer since the 18th century. Besides elegant paper goods, it offers a range of exquisitely sleek leather office accessories.

🍴 EAT

🍴 CANTINETTA DEI VERRAZZANO
Classic Tuscan €€

☎ 055 285 655 590; www.verrazzano.com; Via de' Tavolini 18-20r; ⏰ 8am-9pm Mon-Sat

This one-stop shop for foodies, run by one of Tuscany's great wine-making families, encompasses a gleaming bakery, a wood-burning pizza oven, a cosy dining room serving reasonably priced light Tuscan fare, and (of course) a wine shop. Note the boar meat complete with bristling hide on the walls.

🍴 COCQUINARIUS
Contemporary Tuscan €€

☎ 055 230 21 53; Via delle Oche 15r; ⏰ 9am-11pm Mon-Sat, 9am-4pm Sun, closed Aug

Exposed brick walls are dressed up with antique wine posters at this cosy, informal bar-restaurant. Besides a long wine list, there are creative dishes such as wild boar carpaccio and *tacchino al miele* (turkey with honey) served with a sauce of hazelnuts and sun-dried tomatoes.

🍴 FUSION BAR *Fusion* €€€

☎ 055 272 63; Vicolo dell'Oro 2; ⏰ lunch & dinner

Tucked in the Gallery Art Hotel, this sleek, spacious eatery feels like a high-end furniture shop, complete with Buddha Bar CD. At night sushi rules, but the quirky, reasonable buffet lunch (€16) combines Asia with Tuscany. Think soba noodles next to *mozzarella di bùfala* (mozzarella made from buffalo milk).

🍴 GROM *Gelato*

☎ 055 216 158; www.grom.it; Via del Campanile at Via delle Ocche; ⏱ 10.30am-11pm, until midnight Apr-Sep

Slow food meets gelato. The shop is two parts sterilised dairy, one part 1930s Milan. Top-notch ingredients including seasonal fruits make for remarkable gelati and *sorbetti* (sorbet).Try *crema di Grom,* a confection of cookies and chocolate.

🍴 GUSTAVINO

Contemporary Tuscan   €€€

☎ 055 239 98 06; www.gustavino.it; Via della Condotta 37r; ⏱ lunch & dinner Fri-Sun, dinner only Mon-Thu

Tuscan ingredients undergo a creative makeover inside this glass, stone and steel dining space. Try the ricotta-stuffed artichoke in puff pastry with honeyed pine nuts, or hot chestnuts caramelised in grappa dressed with heavenly *lardo* (yes, pig's lard). The adjacent **La Canova di Gustavino** (☎ 055 239 98 06; Via della Condotta 29r; meals €25; ⏱ noon-11.30pm) serves lighter fair to accompany a long list of Tuscan wines.

Gelato lovers keep the lids rolling at Grom

I FRATELLINI *Quick Eats*   €
☎ 055 239 60 96; Via dei Cimatori 38r;
⏰ 9am-8pm, closed two weeks Aug,
Nov & Feb

Armando and Michele are the gregarious *fratellini* (little brothers) at this great hole in the wall. Costing just a few euros, their made-to-order sandwiches include wild-boar salami with butter, prosciutto with *caperino* (soft goat cheese), and pecorino (a mild cheese made from sheep's milk) with truffle butter. The bread is fresh all day.

OLIVIERO
Italian   €€€
☎ 055 212 421; Via delle Terme 51r;
⏰ dinner Mon-Sat, closed Aug

The kind of place Marcello Mastroianni would have picked at his food if *La Dolce Vita* had been set in Florence, Oliviero is still early 1960s plush with its clubby leather banquettes, sparklingly laid tables, and discreetly formal service. The food, by contrast, is more contemporary, such as the *paparadelle sull'anatra all'arancia* (pasta with duck á l'orange) and meltingly good beef fillet slices served in lard with quail eggs and black truffles.

🍸 DRINK

🍸 CAFFÈ RIVOIRE *Cafe*
⏰ 055 214 412; www.rivoire.it; Piazza della Signoria 4r; ⏰ 8am-midnight Tue-Sun

Maybe the city's choicest location for a cafe, Rivoire charges dearly to sit on its terrace, but your reward

Eager visitors crowd around I Fratellini food and wine stall

is close-up views of Piazza della Signoria, plus the knowledge that you're resting your aching feet while the masses of tourists in view are still on the march.

ⓨ CHIAROSCURO *Cafe*
☎ 055 214 247; Via del Corso 36r; ⏲ 7.30am-9.30pm

With arguably the best coffee in Florence – and that's saying a lot – this casual bar looks more like Soho than Florence with its rough-cut wood interior and kitschy, '60s-style glass chandelier. A variety of excellent beans is available by weight, and the *aperitivo* buffet (6pm to 8pm) makes for a cosy early evening.

ⓨ COLLE BERETTO *Bar/Cafe*
☎ 055 283 156; Piazza Strozzi 5r; ⏲ 11am-3am Tue-Sun

On the same square as the fortress-like Palazzo Strozzi (p48), this bar-cafe opts instead for plate glass and beefy bouncers. The terrace is luxuriously fitted out with cushy sofas, while inside, pea-green neon and transparent Kartell chairs scream design. The *aperitivo* buffet is among the city's most generous.

ⓨ GILLI *Cafe*
☎ 055 213 896; www.gilli.it; Piazza della Repubblica 39r; ⏲ 7am-1am Wed-Mon

At this Florentine institution you can sip your coffee or cocktail beneath Venetian chandeliers and billowy art nouveau ceiling frescoes, or opt for the terrace, with ringside seats on the upscale bustle of Piazza della Repubblica. The elaborate cakes and sweets are also worth a gander.

ⓨ GIUBBE ROSSE *Cafe*
☎ 055 290 052; www.giubberosse.it; Piazza della Repubblica 13/14r; ⏲ 7am-1.30am

The terrace on Piazza della Repubblica looks unpromisingly touristy, but inside the vaulted interior of this fabled, 19th-century cafe Filippo Marinetti and friends dreamed up Italian futurism. Walls are hung with works by generations of past customers, and there are both free foreign-language newspapers and regular literary happenings for the high-minded.

ⓨ JJ CATHEDRAL *Cafe/Bar*
☎ 055 265 68 92; www.jjcathedral.com; Piazza di San Giovanni 4r; ⏲ 10am-2.30am

In the shadow of the Duomo, this classic Irish place spread over two narrow floors has a good selection of draught beers and one truly outstanding draw – a little wrought-iron balcony with cathedral views that are heart-stopping. Jockey early and often if you want to make it your own.

NEIGHBOURHOODS

DUOMO & PIAZZA DELLA SIGNORIA

NEIGHBOURHOODS

DUOMO & PIAZZA DELLA SIGNORIA

EAT, DRINK, MAN, WOMAN: THE APERITIVI HOUR

It used to be that in Florence *aperitivi* meant a pricey before-dinner drink and a few bowls of free crisps and peanuts. However, now bars are battling for the after-work crowd with increasingly elaborate buffets that cost you only the price of one drink.

So far, the marketing ploy has been a screaming success. Drinking is costly in Florence and younger professionals used to go straight home most nights. But most can justify the expense when they can also make a meal of it. And in many places you can do just that, thanks to generous supplies of fresh breads, cheeses and prosciutto, cold and hot pastas, and some kind of fruit or sweet. Now the city is fairly bursting with energy in the early evening. See our favourite venues (p164).

Aperitivi generally start at 7pm and shut down at 10pm. Expect to pay around €10 for that first drink. Remember that the second will cost you just the same. And come early for the best eats, of course.

☿ MAYDAY CLUB *Bar*
☎ 055 238 12 90; www.maydayclub
.it; Via Dante Alighieri 16r; ☯ 8pm-2am
Mon-Sat, closed Aug
Desperate for kitsch that's in good taste? Mayday comes to the rescue with its collection of dolls, model aeroplanes and assorted pop memorabilia hanging neatly from the ceiling. An alternative crowd that tends to be 20-something and English-fluent comes in seeking creative cocktails such as watermelon punch and a cinnamon liqueur with gold shavings.

☿ PROCACCI *Cafe*
☎ 055 211 656; www.antinori.it; Via de' Tornabuoni 64r; ☯ 10.30am-8pm
Tue-Sat
Even the opening hours are genteel at this Florence institution – the last of the old-world cafes on Tornabuoni. And staff actually have the courtesy not to charge you extra to sit down. Founded in 1885, the cafe's wood-panelled interior is reminiscent of a London gentleman's club. Truffles are the order of the day, and a few euros get you a bite-sized *panino tartufato* (truffle pâté sandwich).

☿ SKY LOUNGE *Bar*
☎ 055 272 62; Vicolo dell'Oro 6r;
☯ 8am-2am
Hidden on the top floor of the fashion-forward, Ferragamo-owned Hotel Continentale, the outdoor Sky Lounge offers a modest evening *aperitivo* buffet and spectacular views over the Arno and Florentine rooftops. Doll yourself up to come here or feel out of place.

ⓨ SLOWLY CAFÉ *Bar*
☎ 055 264 53 54; Via Porta Rossa 63r;
🕑 7pm-2.30am Mon-Sat
The pace at Slowly is faster than the name would suggest. The good, daily *aperitivo* buffet attracts a large crowd of single 30-and-ups on the make. Lacking a terrace, it's more popular when weather is inclement, as the well-clad crowds cosy up in the curvaceous leather banquettes and promenade up and down the Lucite stairs.

PLAY
☆ ODEON CINEHALL *Cinema*
☎ 055 295 051; www.cinehall.it; Piazza Strozzi 2
This lovingly restored early 20th-century theatre, complete with intact balcony seats and Tiffany-style cupola, shows films in their original English-language on Monday, Tuesday and Thursday.

☆ TABASCO DISCO GAY *Nightclub*
☎ 055 213 000; www.tabascogay.it; Piazza di Santa Cecilia 3; 🕑 10pm-late
Florence's first and still best gay nightclub gets medieval on your ass, hidden as it is in a catacomb of ancient cellars just off Piazza della Signoria. The music ranges from kitsch to electronica, while the crowd, which starts off gay, turns polymorphous as underground types of all preferences descend after 4am.

☆ YAB CLUB *Nightclub*
☎ 055 215 160; www.yab.it; Via Sassetti 5r
Yes, at YAB, You Are Beautiful, and this sleek, mirror-lined nightclub won't let you forget it. Crowds skew young, and the best sound system in the city centre have made the Monday hip-hop party a Florentine classic.

>SANTA MARIA NOVELLA

Anchored by the ancient and venerable Basilica di Santa Maria Novella, this neighbourhood is a complex stew of super-refined shopping, aristocratic palazzi, uninspired bourgeois apartment blocks and humbler quarters inhabited largely by African and South Asian immigrants. The area around the basilica and adjacent train station has long been the refuge of touts and even dodgier types preying on bewildered tourists. However, the sprucing up of the station, the opening of new high-end hotels and a major facelift for the Piazza di Santa Maria Novella (still in progress at writing) augur more gentrification to come. Already, chic boutiques are proliferating in the area just west of Via de' Tornabuoni, the city's headquarters for luxury shopping. Because it possesses few five-star sights, the neighbourhood is also less heavily touristed, and its back streets are worth a wander for insight into the city of Florence, both ancient and modern.

SANTA MARIA NOVELLA

◎ SEE
Basilica di Santa Maria
  Novella 1 G3
Basilica di Santa Maria
  Novella Entrance 2 G3
Basilica di Santa Trinita...3 H6
Biagiotti Progetto Arte...4 G4
Chiesa d'Ognissanti........5 F4
Chiostri di Santa Maria
  Novella 6 G3
Museo Nazionale Alinari
  della Fotografia 7 G4
Palazzo Rucellai 8 G5
Parco delle Cascine.........9 A1
Ponte Santa Trinita 10 H6
Stazione Santa Maria
  Novella 11 F2

◻ SHOP
Antichi Orologi di Nuti .12 G3
Elio Ferraro...................13 G5
Le Firme........................14 G4
Munstermann 15 F5
Officina Profumo-
  Farmaceutica di Santa
  Maria Novella.............16 F3
Parione 17 H5

▦ EAT
Amon.............................18 F4
Caffè della Spada 19 G4
Caffè Vitali....................20 G4
I Cantinetta Antinori....21 H4
La Martinicca................22 G4

Morione........................23 G4
Rose's............................24 H5

▼ DRINK
Giacosa Roberto
  Cavalli........................25 H5
Noir...............................26 H6
Sei Divino 27 F4

◻ PLAY
Box Office......................28 E1
Central Park...................29 A1
Stazione Leopolda........30 B1
Teatro del Maggio
  Musicale Fiorentino ...31 B3

Please see over for map

SEE

BASILICA DI SANTA MARIA NOVELLA

☎ 055 264 51 84; €2.50; Piazza di Santa Maria Novella; ⏰ 9am-5pm Mon-Thu & Sat, 1-5pm Fri & Sun

The flesh and bones of this Dominican church (see also p20), completed in 1346, may be medieval, but the finishing touches include some of the most seminal works of the Renaissance. Leon Battista Alberti's super-refined facade influenced generations of church architects with its classic motives and balanced geometry. Inside, Masaccio's fresco *Trínita* (Trinity, 1427), on the nave's left flank, is considered the first Renaissance painting, with its distinctly Roman setting and almost perfectly realised, three-dimensional perspective. Note the ominous words of the fresco's skeleton, which translate as 'I was as you are, and you will become as I am.' Its fresco cycles – in particular Filipino Lippi's Cappella Strozzi just right of the altar and Ghirlandaio's Capella Tornabuoni – are also extraordinary. Completed with the help of Michelangelo, Ghirlandaio's cycle depicts the Virgin Maria as a Florentine patrician during the Renaissance, and feature portraits of members of the Tornabuoni family who commissioned it.

BASILICA DI SANTA TRÍNITA

Piazza Santa Trínita; ⏰ 8am-noon, 4-6pm Mon-Sat, 4-6pm Sun

An architectural mishmash that includes a mannerist facade, Romanesque crypt and severe Gothic nave, this often-overlooked church contains Ghirlandaio's Technicolor fresco cycle devoted to St Francis, complete with panoramas of Renaissance Florence.

SANTA MARIA RENOVELLA

The handsomely proportioned piazza in front of the Basilica di Santa Maria Novella has long attracted both pilgrims and those who prey on them. It was begun in the 1280s to accommodate the masses that still come to worship at the basilica. From the 16th to the 19th century, the piazza attracted huge crowds to pageants such as the annual Palio dei Cocchi, a chariot race in which horse and driver raced around the two Egyptian obelisks that still stand at either end of the square.

Touts and pickpockets no doubt made their presence known then, as they do today. Weary tourists fresh off trains from the adjacent Stazione di Santa Maria Novella (p64) make easy targets. However, the piazza is now getting a facelift, including new paving and increased policing. Several high-end hotels and largely respectable bars have opened their doors nearby. And as rents in Florence skyrocket, full-fledged gentrification is merely a matter of time.

BIAGIOTTI PROGETTO ARTE

☎ 055 214 757; www.artbiagiotti.com; Via delle Belle Donne 39r; ⏰ 2-7pm Mon-Sat

On the ground floor of a modest Renaissance palazzo, this simple little art gallery, with its terracotta floors, brick arches and white-washed walls, is one of the city's most stimulating venues for contemporary Italian art.

CHIESA D'OGNISSANTI

Borgo Ognissanti 9; ⏰ 7am-12.30pm, 4-8pm Mon-Sat, 4-8pm Sun

It's hard to believe now, but this church and monastery, which dates to 1256, helped to jumpstart the economy of the nascent city. It was founded by Benedictine monks who brought advanced weaving techniques with them from Lombardy, and Florence went on to make its first fortune in textiles. Today's church is a largely 17th century affair – and a rare example of baroque architecture. Inside the church are works by Botticelli and Ghirlandaio, though the real prize is Ghirlandaio's monumental *Last Supper*. Painted in 1480, it hides within the cloisters to the left of the main entrance.

The Arno with Ponte Santa Trinita and, in the distance, Ponte Vecchio (p50)

CHIOSTRI DI SANTA MARIA NOVELLA

☎ 055 282 187; €2.70; Piazza di Santa Maria Novella; ☽ 9am-5pm Mon-Thu & Sat, 1-5pm Fri & Sun

Hidden off to the left of the Santa Maria Novella's facade, the Chiostro Verde (Green Cloister) takes its name from the green earthen base used for its frescoes. The best are by Paolo Uccello, including the outstanding *Il Diluvio Universale* (Great Flood), from the 1420s. Nearby, the Cappellone degli Spagnoli (Spanish Chapel) is crammed with well-preserved frescoes by Andrea di Bonaiuto from the 1360s. They tell a complex and abstract allegory covering everything from civil law and Pythagorean geometry to the triumph of the Catholic Church.

MUSEO NAZIONALE ALINARI DELLA FOTOGRAFIA

☎ 055 216 310; www.alinari.com/en/museo.asp; adult/student €9/free; Piazza di Santa Maria Novella 14a; ☽ 9.30am-7.30pm Tue-Sun, until 11.30pm Sat

Sheltered incongruously beneath an early Renaissance *loggia* (covered area on the side of a building), this compact, modern museum is the best and brightest addition to the city's art scene in years. It mounts excellent temporary exhibitions, while permanent displays tell the story of Italian and world photography from its invention. The bookshop offers on-demand printing of photos, including many historical photos of Florence, from the renowned Alinari archives.

PALAZZO RUCELLAI

Piazza de' Rucellai

Designed by Leon Battista Alberti in the 1440s for one of Florence's richest families, this palazzo is arguably the first Renaissance building to rigorously mimic Roman forebearers – in this case, the Colosseum, with its Doric, Ionic and Corinthian pilasters. Note that the interior is not open to visitors.

PARCO DELLE CASCINE

Just outside the city's ancient gates begins a long, leafy and appropriately lung-shaped park. Once the Medicis' private hunting grounds, its 100-plus hectares encompass jogging trails, a public pool, and the city's biggest nightclub (p70).

PONTE SANTA TRÍNITA

Composed of three elliptical arches of the utmost elegance – the first of their kind ever used in bridge construction – Ponte Santa Trínita was designed in the 1560s by Ammannati, though its arches, reminiscent of the tombs in Cappelle Medicee (p77), have lead some to suspect Michelangelo's

GIORGIO VASARI: PRO OR CON?

Giorgio Vasari (1511–74) takes a lot of flack from art historians, and for good reason. He painted over medieval frescoes in a drive to 'purify' the art in Florentine churches, including Santa Maria Novella. It's also believed he painted over unfinished works by Leonardo da Vinci and Michelangelo in the Palazzo Vecchio (p48) in order to make way for a bombastic fresco cycle glorifying the Medici who paid all his bills – Duke Cosimo I.

At the same time, Vasari's pioneering series of biographies called *Le Vite delle più eccellenti pittori, scultori, ed architettori* (Lives of the Most Excellent Painters, Sculptors, and Architects) are still the basic text of Renaissance art studies. In fact, he even coined the very term 'Renaissance'. Ironically, his own art is considered mannerist – a style that drew on Renaissance innovations but added self-conscious distortions, jarring scales and unlikely juxtapositions that shatter the Renaissance drive for balance, harmony and naturalism.

Though his paintings were greatly admired in his own times, they generally evoke yawns today. The perspective and modelling are skilful, but they somehow suffer from a certain spiritual flatness. However, his architectural works still win high marks. Perhaps his greatest work, the light-filled, U-shaped Palazzo (now Galleria) degli Uffizi (p10), is a wildly inventive building that both encloses its central plaza and leaves it permeable to the rest of the city.

hand. Destroyed by Nazi bombs in 1944, it was reconstructed from the original stones retrieved from the Arno.

STAZIONE DI SANTA MARIA NOVELLA

Most people rush through Florence's main station without a second glance, but in fact it's one of Italy's great Modernist buildings, if not to all tastes. Built in the early 1930s, the station's plain facade mimics the rough stone of churches such as San Lorenzo (p73), while the red-and-white striped marble floors recall the city's official colours. In the understated but ultrarefined main hall, a combination of sharp, aerodynamic lines and

wide marble expanses give a sense of both speed and solidity.

SHOP

ANTICHI OROLOGI DI NUTI
Accessories
☎ 055 294 594; Via della Scala 10r;
🕑 9am-12.30pm, 4-7.30pm Tue-Sun
Step back in time, literally, at this small but exquisite shop that is ticking with antique timepieces, from Empire table clocks to art deco watches.

ELIO FERRARO *Clothing*
☎ 055 292 993; www.elioferraro.com; Via del Parione 47r
The queen of vintage, Elio woos vintage lovers with her retro

1950s and 1960s couture, fashion accessories and Italian furniture – all designer-made, of course, darling, and with the price tags to match.

LE FIRME *Clothing*
☎ 055 291 843; Piazza di Santa Maria Novella

It may look disorderly, even down at the heels, but this shop is crowded with great deals on last season's fashions for both men and women.

MUNSTERMANN
Pharmacy
☎ 055 210 660; www.munstermann.it; Piazza Carlo Goldoni 2r

Unapologetically 19th century, this grand old pharmacy still brews up its own herbal remedies, natural fragrances and cosmetics. Scents include Tuscan lavender, Florentine iris and *agrumi* – a sweetly bracing citrus concoction.

OFFICINA PROFUMO-FARMACEUTICA DI SANTA MARIA NOVELLA
Pharmacy
☎ 055 216 276; Via della Scala 16

Need some baroque frippery to go with your jar of skin cream? This extraordinary shop, which is spread out over a series of palatial rooms, feels more like a museum

than a commercial outfit with its medieval frescoes and elaborately carved glass-front cabinets. It began its life as the apothecary of the Santa Maria Novella, when monks concocted cures in its herb garden. In 1612 it opened its doors to the public, and it still offers Renaissance remedies – acqua di Santa Maria Novella to cure hysterics, acqua di Melissa to aid digestion, even smelling salts. All of its products remain top-notch, though today they include modern necessities such as eye cream and room spray.

A letter writer's heaven at Parione (p66)

NEIGHBOURHOODS

SANTA MARIA NOVELLA

FASHIONISTA FIORENTINA

While Via de' Tornabuoni has recently turned into a mini-mecca for fashionistas from around the world, Florence has in fact made a living off producing fancy threads for nearly a millennium. The city established itself as a centre of fine woollen textiles in the Middle Ages, a market it dominated for four centuries. Even today, many top designers make seasonal pilgrimages from Paris and New York to buy first-quality fabrics from Florentine factories. At the same time, many of the bags and shoes from the likes of Prada and Fendi are frequently crafted in dime-sized, independent workshops found in and around Florence.

The city is also considered the birthplace of contemporary Italian fashion, thanks to a legendary series of shows staged by Giovanni Battista Giorgini in 1951. He introduced the world to fellow Florentine aristocrat Emilio Pucci and other designers who gave a bold, new twist to the prevailing Parisian 'New Look' of Chanel and Dior.

Today, some of the biggest Milanese brands have Florentine origins. Guccio Gucci (1881–1953) started out as an Oltrarno saddle-maker before turning to shoes and hand-bags. Local son Roberto Cavalli (born 1940) is renowned for his envelope-pushing fabrics, animal prints and sensual cuts. And Salvatore Ferragamo (1898–1960) won over Hollywood and the world by turning shoes into objets d'art. See a selection of these at the Museo Ferragamo (p46).

🖼 PARIONE *Stationery*
☎ 055 215 684; www.parione.it; Via dei Parione 10r
Stocked with flowery stationery, fountain pens and hand-made miniatures of antique desks and bookshelves, this classically Florentine stationer makes you long for a return to a world before email.

EAT

🍴 AMON *Middle Eastern* €
☎ 055 293 146; Via Palazzuolo 26r;
🕙 noon-3pm, 6-11pm
Pop in to this family-run joint for what are possibly the best kebabs in Florence. Refreshingly nongreasy, they're served on pita bread fresh from the oven. Admire the Egyptian kitsch on the walls while you wait.

🍴 CAFFÈ DELLA SPADA
Classic Tuscan €€
☎ 055 218 757; Via della Spada 62r;
🕙 lunch & dinner
This classic Florentine *rosticceria* (shop serving roast meat and other cooked items) serves spit-roasted meats and other prepared dishes such as lentil stew, roasted eggplant and sauteed spinach, all packed neatly for take-away. Or you can sit in one of a pair of rustic

dining rooms, decked out with countrified terracotta floors and wood-beamed ceilings. Be prepared to wait to sit, as fair prices attract big crowds.

🍽 CAFFÈ VITALI *Italian* €€
☎ 055 285 486; Via del Moro 51r;
🕐 8am-8pm Mon-Sat, closed Aug

A rare good-value place in this stretch of Florence, this recently spruced up restaurant and wine bar has a surprising amount of class for the price, with art in gilded frames and wood-panelled walls. The menu is standard Italian fare prepared with care. Try the gnocchi in a rich sea of smoked cheeses.

🍽 I CANTINETTA ANTINORI
Classic Tuscan €€€
☎ 055 235 98 27; www.antinori.it;
Piazza degli Antinori 3; 🕐 lunch & dinner Mon-Fri

Tuscany's most famous wine-making dynasty has given over a portion of their Renaissance city home for oenophiles who want a full meal to accompany their tipple. Ask the bow-tied waiters what pourings go best with classic Tuscan dishes such as *bistecca alla fiorentina* (p21) and *trippa alla fiorentina* (tripe Florentine-style). Afterwards view models of the family's Tuscan, Umbrian and Californian wine-producing estates in the palazzo's courtyard.

A stroll down fashionable Via de' Tornabuoni reveals a bounty of shops and galleries

Neri Torrigiani
Graphic designer, impresario, debonair man-about-town

Like so many Florentines, Neri Torrigiani's job is to make lovely things even more lovely, from Gucci galas to Prada packaging. His special passion: Tuscany's craftspeople, whom he fetes each May with a week-long event called Artigianato e Palazzo (www.artigianatoepalazzo.it). Torrigiani's family has been integral to Florentine history since medieval times. Not surprising, then, that he personifies the city's peculiar genius in marrying apparent opposites such as beauty and entrepreneurship, sophistication and rustic simplicity. For a discreet meal with clients, he heads to the Zenlike serenity of trendy Rose's (opposite). But he is equally happy with a tripe sandwich from his favourite stand near Porta Romana. Torrigiani's tip for indulging *la dolce vita* Florence-style: La Dolce Vita (p136) of course. 'It's right on the piazza, so people can drive up in their sports cars. Lots of space to display all the trappings of the ego.'

🍴 LA MARTINICCA
Classic Tuscan €€

☎ 055 218 928; Via del Sole 27r;
🕐 lunch & dinner Mon-Fri, dinner only Sat & Sun

This family-run trattoria looks dowdy with its lace curtains and overly cosy dining room. But local foodies praise the loving preparation and adherence to tradition in its homemade pastas, *risotto allo zafferano* (saffron risotto) and a celebrated chocolate and pistachio torte.

🍴 MORIONE
Classic Tuscan €€€

☎ 055 239 61 73; Via Palazzuolo 56r;
🕐 9am-2pm, 3-7pm Mon-Tue, Thu-Sat, 3-7pm Wed

Hats off to this neat-as-a-pin purveyor of fresh pastas, including ravioli fixing to burst with fresh vegetables and top-quality meats and cheeses. A wall of plate glass reveals Signor Morione at work on his creations.

🍴 ROSE'S *Fusion* €€€

☎ 055 287 090; www.roses.it; Via del Parione 26r; 🕐 noon-1.30am Mon-Sat

The name doesn't suggest sushi, but in the evenings this serene little restaurant-cafe, which looks like a prettied-up Zen monastery, serves up some of the best in town. Lunches are light and are, by contrast, very much Tuscan

affairs, with top-notch salads and sandwiches that seem designed to keep figures slim for fittings at the designer shops on nearby Via de' Tornabuoni.

🍸 DRINK

🍸 NOIR *Bar*

Lungarno Corsini 12-14r; 🕐 11am-2am

Noir is the new black. Set in a riverside palazzo, the bar's interior lives up to its name. Except for the original baroque fresco gracing one of its ceilings, everything is black as night, from the walls and light fixtures to the high-back velvet banquettes. Designer labels figure prominently at its generous *aperitivo* buffet when, in warm weather, crowds spill out onto the Arno's banks.

🍸 GIACOSA ROBERTO CAVALLI *Bar/Cafe*

☎ 055 211 656; Via della Spada 10r;
🕐 9am-11pm Mon-Sat

Once the hub of Anglo-Florentine sophistication during the interwar years, this tiny but venerable cafe has gotten an extreme makeover from its new owner Roberto Cavalli, whose flagship store sits next door. Think fake Zebra-skin picture frames, fake leopard-skin ottomans and a surgically enhanced clientele. The sidewalk terrace seating makes for great people-watching.

NEIGHBOURHOODS

SANTA MARIA NOVELLA

 SEI DIVINO *Cafe*
☎ 055 217 791; Borgo Ognissanti 42r;
⏰ 8am-2am
Besides booze, this casual wine
and cocktail bar serves up wi-fi, a
two-course lunch (€8) and a nightly
aperitivi buffet that includes Mexi-
can on Monday, sushi on Tuesday
and vegetarian on Wednesday.

⭐ PLAY
⭐ **BOX OFFICE** *Cinema*
☎ 055 210 804; www.boxol.it, in Italian;
Via Luigi Alamanni 39; ⏰ 3.30-7.30pm
Mon, 10am-7.30pm Tue-Sat
Tickets for the lion's share of the
city's cultural events are sold at this
central outlet. Plan to bring cash –
credit cards are not accepted.

⭐ **CENTRAL PARK** *Nightclub*
☎ 055 353 505; Via Fosso Macinante 2;
⏰ 11pm-6am Tue-Sat
Hidden off in the leafy Parco delle
Cascine, Florence's largest disco
brings several acres of Ibiza to the
city's western edge. The sprawling
club has two outdoor dance floors,
an artificial waterfall, VIP lounge
seating raised a metre or so above
the common folk, plus a pair of
indoor dance floors. Move back
and forth between pop, dance,
electronica or disco kitsch, as the
mood dictates.

Taking a little time out at Giacosa Roberto Cavalli (p69)

SLOW TRAIN COMING

In a bid to reduce the estimated one million cars on its overloaded streets, Florence is in the process of installing 'super trams' – known as Tramvia – to link its increasingly sprawling suburbs with its increasingly congested historic centre. Like all good things in Florence, the tram project comes freighted with both virulent polemics and 'unanticipated' delays. Those living along the construction complain about noise and increased traffic delays, while art historians have lobbied hard against a proposal to lay tracks all the way to the Duomo, which they say will compromise ancient buildings. Continuation of the project was brought to a vote in a citywide referendum in early 2008. It lost. However, the vote was not legally binding and authorities vow that work will continue anyway. The first line, which heads southwest across the Arno from the centre, should be completed by 2009. At writing it still remains to be determined whether a second line will penetrate the city's historic core.

⭐ **STAZIONE LEOPOLDA**
Arts Centre
Viale Fratelli Roselli
Long abandoned, the city's once-grand train station has won a second lease on life as a cultural centre that is best known for its Fabbrica Europa festival (p28), which attracts avant-garde artists and performers from all over Europe. It's located near the eastern end of Parco delle Cascine just outside the Porta di Prato city gates.

⭐ **TEATRO DEL MAGGIO MUSICALE FIORENTINO** *Theatre*
☎ 055 27 793 50, tickets 055 287 2 22; www.maggiofiorentino.com;
Corso Italia 16
The curtain rises on opera, classical concerts and ballet at this theatre, also known as the Teatro Comunale, located outside the western edge of the historic centre. The theatre also serves as the principle venue for the Maggio Musicale Fiorentino international concert festival in May and June (p28).

>SAN LORENZO

Long the stomping grounds of the Medici family, this busy, commercial neighbourhood is bounded on one side by the Palazzo Medici-Riccardi (p78), the family's first grand city home, and on the other by the Fortezza da Basso (p78), the fort they built to remind their fellow citizens exactly who was in charge. And at its heart lies the ethereally beautiful Basilica di San Lorenzo (opposite), where for centuries the Medici buried their dead and still wow the living due to their far-sighted patronage of the likes of Brunelleschi and Michelangelo. The nearby Mercato Centrale (p82) offers up the best produce of Tuscany's farms, while the streets are clogged with merchants hawking leather and other goods, often of more dubious quality. It may be the least picturesque neighbourhood in central Florence with its snarled streets and quantity of tatty shops and hotels, but its individual parts are remarkable.

SAN LORENZO

Please see over for map

SEE

BASILICA DI SAN LORENZO

☎ 055 264 51 84; €3.50; Piazza San Lorenzo; ⏰ 10am-5.30pm Mon-Sat, 1-5.30pm Sun Mar-Oct

Founded in the late 4th-century, San Lorenzo lays claim to being the oldest church in Florence and once served as its cathedral, though the current incarnation dates to the 1420s, when the Medicis hired Brunelleschi to spruce up their parish church. The facade may look like a pile of rough-cut stones, but it belies the extraordinary, light-filled interior. The harmonious geometry, quantities of natural light and classical Corinthian columns of

pietra serena (soft grey stone) were unlike anything in Christendom. Michelangelo was commissioned to design the facade in 1518, though it was never executed, hence its unfinished appearance. Donatello, who sculpted the church's two bronze pulpits, is buried in the chapel featuring Fra Filippo Lippi's *Annunciation*. Also look for Rosso Fiorentino's *Sposalizio della Vergine* (Marriage of the Virgin Mary; 1523) with its handsome young Joseph, and Bronzino's gruesomely vivid fresco of the martyrdom of Saint Lawrence, the church's namesake. Left of the altar lies the outstanding **Sagrestia Vecchia** (Old Sacristy), also designed by Brunelleschi.

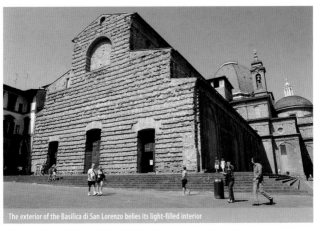

The exterior of the Basilica di San Lorenzo belies its light-filled interior

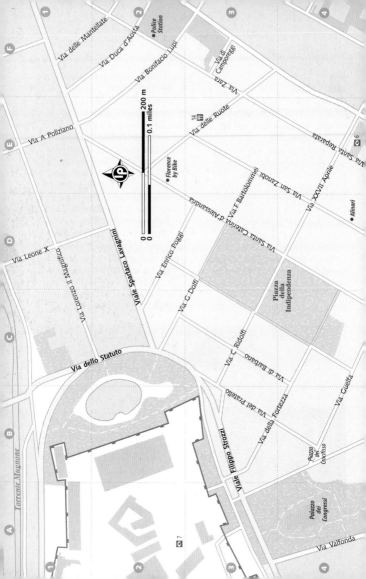

Police Station

Via delle Martellate

Via Duca d'Aosta

Via Bonifacio Lupi

Via di Camporeggi

Via Zara

Via A. Poliziano

Via delle Ruote

14

Florence by Bike

Via Santa Reparata

Via San Zanobi

Via F. Bartolommei

Via XXVII Aprile

Alinari

Via Leone X

Via Lorenzo il Magnifico

Viale Spartaco Lavagnini

Via Enrico Poggi

Via Santa Caterina d'Alessandria

Via dello Statuto

Via G. Dolfi

Piazza della Indipendenza

Torrente Mugnone

Via C. Ridolfi

Via di Barbano

Via Guelfa

Via del Pratello

Via della Fortezza

Viale Filippo Strozzi

Piazza del Crocifisso

Palazzo dei Congressi

Via Valfonda

200 m

0   0.1 miles

7

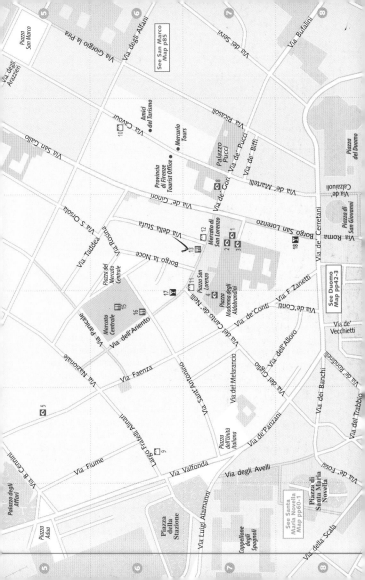

Piazza San Marco

Via degli Arazzieri

Via Giorgio la Pira

Via degli Alfani

See San Marco
Map p85

Via dei Servi

Via Bufalini

Via San Gallo

Via Cavour

10

Amid
del Turismo

Mercurio
Tours

Via Ricasoli

Via de' Pucci

Palazzo
Pucci

Piazza
del Duomo

Via de' Biffi

Provincia
di Firenze
Tourist Office

Via de' Cironi

Via de' Conti

8

Via de' Martelli

Via de' Calzaiuoli

Piazza di
San Giovanni

Via S. Orsola

Via della Stufa

Via Rosina

Mercato di
San Lorenzo

12

Borgo la Noce

13

Via Taddea

Piazza del
Mercato
Centrale

11

1

Piazza San
Lorenzo

2 3

Via Roma

Borgo San Lorenzo

18

See Duomo
Map pp42-3

Mercato
Centrale

15

17

4

Piazza
Madonna degli
Aldobrandini

Via de' Cerretani

16

Via dell'Ariento

Via del Canto de' Nelli

Via de' Conti

Via de' Conti

Via de' Vecchietti

Via Panicale

Via Nazionale

Via Faenza

Via dei Melarancio

Via dell'Alloro

Via del Giglio

Via F Zanetti

Via de' Banchi

Via de' Rondinelli

Via Sant'Antonino

5

Piazza
dell'Unità
Italiana

Via de' Panzani

Via de' Fossi

Largo Fratelli Alinari

Via Fiume

9

Via Valfonda

Via degli Avelli

See Santa
Maria Novella
Map pp60-1

Via B Cennini

Palazzo degli
Affari

Piazza
Adua

Piazza
della
Stazione

Via Luigi Alamanni

Cappellone
degli
Spagnoli

Piazza di
Santa Maria
Novella

Via de' Trabbio

Via della Scala

OLD FOX

Throughout the Middle Ages and Renaissance, political life in Florence was rife with factionalism as various wealthy families vied for dominance. Civil strife led to the exile of some of its greatest figures, from Dante to Machiavelli. However, the ever wily Cosimo il Vecchio (1389–1464), founder of the Medici political dynasty, managed to turn even his exile to his advantage by taking much of the city's banking business with him. After winning his return, he proceeded to win over the populace by negotiating peace with natural enemies such as Milan and Venice. At the same time, he was always careful to pay lip service to the city's republican institutions and maintain a certain personal austerity.

Many historians argue that the stability Cosimo imposed helped foster the Renaissance. Certainly, his generous support of the arts was key. He commissioned works by, among others, Fra Angelico, Filippo Lippi and Donatello. And to the San Lorenzo district, which was his family stomping grounds, he added two of Florence's most revolutionary buildings, Michelozzo's Palazzo Medici-Riccardi (p78) and Brunelleschi's Basilica di San Lorenzo (p73).

📖 BIBLIOTECA MEDICEA-LAURENZIANA
☎ 055 211 590; €3.50; www.bml .firenze.sbn.it; Piazza San Lorenzo 9; ⏰ 9.30am-1.30pm Sun-Fri
Hidden at the end of the cloister just to the left of San Lorenzo's main entrance, this library was founded by Medici pope Clement VII in the 1520s for the safekeeping of his family's invaluable collection of books and manuscripts. Architectural historians go gaga over the mannerist-style vestibule and reading room designed by Michelangelo. He borrowed materials and motifs from Brunelleschi's adjacent church yet breaks rule after architectural rule, using for example structural elements that serve no structural purpose and crowding decorative elements so

that they are crowded to overlapping. The effect is a kind of sublime unease, almost claustrophobia.

🏛 CAPPELLA DEI MAGI
☎ 055 276 03 40; www.palazzo-medici .it; €5 (including entrance to the palazzo); Palazzo Medici-Riccardi; Via Cavour 3; ⏰ 9am-7pm Thu-Tue
Also known as Capella di Benozzo, this tiny chapel flaunts a series of wonderfully detailed serene frescoes (1459) by Benozzo Gozzoli, a pupil of Fra Angelico. The ostensible theme of Journey of the Magi is but a slender pretext for portraying members of the Medici clan in their best light; try to spy Lorenzo il Magnifico, Cosimo il Vecchio and the artist's self-portrait in the crowd. Only eight visitors are allowed in at a time for

a maximum of just seven minutes; reserve your slot in advance at the palace ticket desk.

CAPPELLE MEDICEE
☎ 055 238 86 02; Piazza Madonna degli Aldobrandini; €6; ⏲ 8.15am-1.50pm Tue-Sat & 2nd & 4th Mon of month, 8.15am-5.50pm 1st, 3rd & 5th Sun

Nowhere is Medici conceit expressed so explicitly as in their mausoleum. The soaring and rather overblown main chapel is sumptuously adorned in baroque style with granite, marble and semiprecious stones. From here a corridor leads to the stark Sagrestia Nuova (New Sacristy), Michelangelo's first architectural work and showcase for three of his most haunting sculptures.

Aurora e Crepusculo (Dawn and Dusk) lounges on the sarcophagus of the unpopular Lorenzo Duke of Urbino (1492–1519) to whom Machiavelli dedicated *The Prince*. *Notte e Giorno* (Night and Day) marks the spot opposite where a son of Lorenzo il Magnifico is buried. The unfinished tomb of Lorenzo il Magnifico is simply adorned with a serene *Madonna col Bambino* (Madonna and Child). Like his Biblioteca Medicea-Laurenziana (opposite), the room borrows from Brunelleschi but subtly unsettles the viewer with its empty niches, overlapping decorative elements and the precarious way the monumental figures of Dawn, Dusk, Day and Night are perched on their curved pedestals.

Marvel at he Medicis' elaborate mausoleum -- the Michelangelo-designed Cappelle Medicee

◎ CENACOLO DEL CONSERVATORIO DI FULIGNO

☎ 055 286 982; Via Faenza 42;
⏱ 9am-noon Tue, Thu & Sat

In 1845 workers in an ex-convent uncovered an extraordinary site – a huge, intact fresco of the Last Supper in a former monk's dining room. At first attributed to Raphael, it is now generally believed to be the work of Perugino, though completed largely by his students. The dining apostles are set against a sylvan country scene, creating the effect that you're looking through a window onto the harmonious scene.

◎ CENACOLO DI SANT'APOLLONIA

☎ 055 238 86 07; Via XXVII Aprile 1;
⏱ 8.15am-1.50pm Tue-Sat, 1st, 3rd & 5th Mon, 2nd & 4th Sun

Once part of a sprawling Benedictine monastery, this *cenacolo* (monk's dining room) harbours arguably the city's most remarkable Last Supper scene. Painted by Andrea del Castagno in the 1440s, it is one of the first works of its kind to effectively apply Renaissance perspective. It possesses a haunting power with its vivid colours – especially the almost abstract squares of marble painted above the apostles' heads – as well as the dark, menacing figure of Judas.

◎ FORTEZZA DA BASSO

Vialle Fillippo Strozi

Now a conference centre, this Renaissance fort dates to the 1530s, when the recently restored Medicis felt it best to intimidate their own restive population. Note that the pentagonal fort is only open to conference attendees.

◎ PALAZZO MEDICI-RICCARDI

☎ 055 276 03 40; www.palazzo-medici .it; €5 (including Cappella dei Magi); Via Cavour 3; ⏱ 9am-7pm Thu-Tue

By the 1440s, Cosimo il Vecchio had consolidated control in Florence, so he commissioned Michelozzo to build a city home befitting his new status. With the fortresslike houses of medieval Florence no longer necessary, Michelozzo set about to invent an entirely new kind of building. His palazzo became a blueprint of aristocratic Florentine residences, and its influence is clear in the Palazzo Pitti, Palazzo Strozzi and Palazzo Rucellai. The rusticated facade of the ground floor gives a rather stern aspect to the building, though the upper two storeys are less aggressive, maintaining restrained classical lines and topped with a heavy timber roof whose broad eaves protrude over the street below. The most remarkable feature of the interior is its Cappella dei Magi (p76).

Marco Mazzoni
Modern dancer, founding member of Kinkaleri art collective

Known for its iconoclastic shows that mix dance, theatre and projected images, Kinkaleri (www.kinkaleri.it) is a growing force in Florence's avant-garde art scene. Like any good Dadaist, Marco Mazzoni, a founding member of the collective, takes special delight in inverting expectations, so when asked to name his favourite spot in Florence, he mentions the last of the free street parking near ex-Stazione Leopolda (p71) in a city awash in cars. **Does the weight of the Renaissance weigh on a contemporary artist like a burden?** 'No', says Marco, 'because those we consider the masters – Donatello, Ghiberti and Brunelleschi – were in fact extremely subversive. But it takes an act of the imagination for us to remember that now.' To ensure he is not freighted by the past, the only museum Marco regularly visits is the Museo Zoologico La Specola (p113), where he draws inspiration from wax sculptures of human autopsies.

🛍 SHOP

📷 ARCHIVI FOTOGRAFICI ALINARI *Photographs*

☎ 055 239 51; www.alinari.com; Largo Fratelli Alinari 15; 🕙 9am-1pm, 2-6pm Mon-Fri, closed two weeks mid-Aug

The world's oldest photographic firm has, since its founding in 1852, amassed an archive of some 3.5 million photographs, ranging from daguerreotypes to digital images. The firm began by specialising in art and architecture, but has expanded to documentary-style photographs. The archives are open to the public, and you can still order prints of the original photographs just like Lucy Honeychurch in *A Room with a View*. The archives also form the nucleus of the collection at the nearby Museo Nazionale Alinari della Fotografia (p63).

📷 JOHNSON & RELATIVES *Stationery*

☎ 055 265 81 03; Via Cavour 49r

An offshoot of Giulio Giannini & Figlio (p128), this cosy little shop on a busy thoroughfare has a distinctly Victorian-era flavour. Besides Giannini's classic Florentine stationery products, you can buy loose leaves of hand-marbled paper, antique postcards and prints, and clever objets d'art.

Meat-free dining at Il Vegetariano

NEIGHBOURHOODS

FAT CHANCE

While most of us are doing our best to cut animal fat out of our diets, Florentine cooks work eagerly to add it back into theirs. Not any fat will do, though. The real prize is *lardo di Colonnata*, cured pig's fat from Tuscany's mountainous northwest corner. The fat is placed in marble tubs that have been rubbed in garlic and then immersed in a briny concoction of sea salt, herbs and spices. In six to 10 months, it will be ready for you to slather onto warm toast or polenta. The unctuous delicacy will literally melt in your mouth.

SAN LORENZO

MERCATO SAN LORENZO
Leather
☎ 055 214 795; Piazza San Lorenzo & around; ⏰ 9.30am-7.30pm Tue-Sun

With stalls radiating out in all directions from the Basilica di San Lorenzo, this street market has mostly second-rate knock-offs of classic Florentine crafts, from leather jackets to marbled paper. If you're after boxer briefs superimposed with an image of David's crotch, this is also your spot. Those willing to bargain can generally negotiate good deals.

PASSAMANERIA TOSCANA
Furnishings
☎ 055 214 670; www.passmaneriatoscana.com; Piazza San Lorenzo 12r

Specialising in brocade textiles in classical Florentine style, this one-of-a-kind shop is heavily laden with tassels, pillowcases, bed covers and wall hangings. It may have a workaday air, but the fabrics are top-notch. A must if you want to recreate that Medici look back home.

EAT

DA SERGIO
Classic Tuscan €€
☎ 055 281 941; Piazza San Lorenzo 8r; ⏰ lunch Mon-Sat, closed Aug

The clientele at this rustic eatery tucked behind the stalls of the Mercato San Lorenzo includes large numbers of old Florentine men dining solo – the ultimate sign of a real trattoria. The handwritten menu includes Tuscan classics such as *minestra di farro* (spelt soup) and *bistecca alla fiorentina* (p21).

IL VEGETARIANO
Vegetarian €€
☎ 055 47 50 30; Via delle Ruote 30r; meals €15; ⏰ lunch Tue-Fri, lunch & dinner Sat & Sun, closed Aug; Ⓥ

This self-service veggie restaurant cooks up a great selection of Tuscan vegetable dishes, build-your-own salads and mains eaten around shared wooden tables. There's always a vegan option and the chalked-up menu changes daily.

🍴 MERCATO CENTRALE
Self-catering €

Piazza del Mercato Centrale; ⏱ 7am-2pm Mon-Sat

Inside an iron-and-glass structure dating to 1874 lies the oldest and largest food market in Florence. Stalls on the 1st floor are devoted to fresh meat and fish as well as *salumi* (prepared meats), cheeses, fresh pasta, olive oils, jams, truffle butter and more. For the pride of Tuscan produce, head upstairs to the mezzanine. You may have to negotiate through a confusion of makeshift stands of clothes and leathergoods to reach the market.

🍴 NERBONE
Classic Tuscan €

☎ 055 219 949; Mercato Centrale, Piazza del Mercato Centrale; ⏱ 7am-2pm Mon-Sat

Crowds queue for lunchtime platters of *trippa alla fiorentina* (tripe and tomato stew), tripe *panini* and *panini con bollito,* a boiled beef bun infamously dipped in the cooking pot immediately before serving (no, it's not soggy incredibly). Dine standing up or around a handful of tables.

🍸 DRINK

🍸 CASA DEL VINO *Wine Bar*

☎ 055 215 609; Via dell'Ariento 16r; ⏱ 9.30am-4pm Mon-Sat, closed Aug

Locals keep popping in all day long for a nip or two from a limited but carefully selected list of daily pourings of Chianti at this quintessential Florentine *enoteca* (wine bar). Its carved wooden cabinetry, no-nonsense service and mini-panini round out the happy picture.

🍸 NANNINI COFFEE SHOP
Cafe

☎ 055 212 680; Via Borgo San Lorenzo 7r; ⏱ 7am-9pm

At the cheerful, Florentine branch of a legendary Sienese bakery,

---

A LOAD OF TRIPE

Florentines are sometimes accused of frugality. That's certainly true when it comes to the cow, of which they waste very little. You can, for example, purchase *pulmone* – a nice fat cow's lung – at the butchers of the Mercato Centrale (above). And when time and/or money are short, Florentines head happily to the nearest *trippaio* – usually a mobile van or wheeled cart – for a juicy tripe burger. Think cow's stomach chopped up, boiled, sliced and stuffed into a bun. For extra bite, they add a dash *salsa verde* (pea-green sauce of smashed parsley, garlic, capers and anchovies) or *salsa piccante* (chilli sauce). Not for you? How about a bowl of *lampredotto* – the cow's fourth stomach chopped and simmered for a day or so.

Sample what a Florentine *enoteca* (wine bar) is all about at Casa del Vino

you'll find classics such as *cantuc-cini* (almond biscuits), *ricciarelli* (chocolate-covered marzipan petits fours), and *panforte* (a sweet concoction of nuts, spices and fruit). Nannini's renowned home-roasted coffees are also definitely worth sampling.

>SAN MARCO

Taking its name from the illustrious monastery at its heart, this small neighbourhood north of the Duomo is a dense mix of shops, university buildings and commercial offices hidden discretely within Renaissance-style palazzi. The vast majority of visitors come here for one reason: to gawk at the neighbourhood's most famous resident: Michelangelo's *David*. He has made his home here since 1873, when the city built him the theatrically neoclassical Galleria dell'Accademia (p87). Just a block away, the Museo di San Marco (p89) harbours a precious stash of works by the monastery's most illustrious brother, Fra Angelico. Also nearby, the *loggia* (covered area on the side of a building) of the Spedale degli Innocenti (p90) is often called the first Renaissance building for its conscious imitation of Roman architectural forms. Finally, there are also smaller wonders, such as the trompe l'oeil mosaics in the Opificio delle Pietre Dure (p89) and the Etruscan collection at the Museo Archeologico (p88).

SAN MARCO

◉ SEE
Chiesa della Santissima
   Annunziata.................**1** C2
Chiesa di San Marco .....(see 6)
Chiostro dello Scalzo......**2** C1
Galleria dell'Accademia .**3** B2
Giardino dei Semplici.....**4** D1
Museo Archeologico.......**5** C2
Museo di San Marco.......**6** B1
Opificio delle
   Pietre Dure.................**7** B2
Spedale degli
   Innocenti....................**8** C2

🍴 EAT
Caffellatte **9** D4
Carabè **10** B3
Il Pizzicagnolo **11** D4
Oile Shoppe **12** C4
Oliandolo.....................**13** B3
Ruth's **14** E4

🍷 DRINK
La Mescita **15** C3
La Robiglio **16** C3
Rex Caffè **17** D4

★ PLAY
Be Bop Music Club........**18** C3
Jazz Club......................**19** D4
Teatro della Pergola.....**20** D4

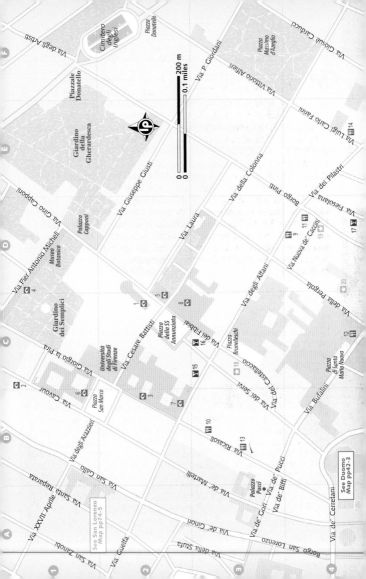

👁 SEE

📷 CHIESA DELLA SANTISSIMA ANNUNZIATA

☎ 055 266 181; Piazza della Santissima Annunziata; ⏰ 7.30am-12.30pm & 4-6.30pm

Established in 1250 by the founders of the Servite order and rebuilt by Michelozzo and others in the mid-15th century, this Renaissance church is most remarkable for the post-Renaissance painters who worked here together and helped found the mannerist school. There are frescoes by Andrea del Castagno in the first two chapels on the left of the church, and the frescoes in Michelozzo's atrium include work by del Sarto as well as Jacopo Pontormo and Il Rosso Fiorentino (the Redhead from Florence). Also look for the fresco by Perugino in the fifth chapel and a mosaic lunette of the Annunciation by Davide Ghirlandaio, Domenico's little brother, above the main entrance.

📷 CHIOSTRO DELLO SCALZO

☎ 055 238 86 04; Via Cavour 69; ⏰ 8.15am-1.50pm Mon, Thu & Sat

Painted for a Catholic brotherhood that showed its faith by going barefoot (scalzo), Andrea del Sarto's monochromatic fresco cycle is ranged around a Renaissance cloister of unlikely elegance, considering the brotherhood's professions of humility. Completed between 1509 and 1526, the cycle depicts the life of St John the Baptist in 16 scenes – all in shades of grey. The ensemble also reveals del Sarto's

UP IN FLAMES

As the Medicis were losing their grip on Florence in the 1490s, the Dominican monk Girolamo Savonarola was drawing sell-out crowds with his fiery sermons. His apocalyptic vision was appealing since the city's fortunes had been badly damaged by French-Italian wars that threatened to get worse. And his attacks on material luxury appealed to Florentines who watched Renaissance bankers build increasingly elaborate monuments to their own wealth.

When the Medicis were forced into exile in 1494, Savonarola effectively ran the city, which he renamed 'a Christian and religious republic'. During the famous Bonfire of the Vanities of 1497, his followers went house to house to collect pagan books, 'immoral' art, even mirrors and musical instruments, which were ritually burned in the Piazza della Signoria. It's said works by Michelangelo and Botticelli also went up in flames.

Savonarola's extremism eventually drew the wrath of the pope, himself a worldly man, and on 23 May 1498 the monk met the same fate as the books he burned when he, too, was put to the stake in Piazza della Signoria. His executioners made sure there was nothing left but ashes, for fear that his followers would turn chards of bone into relics.

The Giardino dei Semplici offers a pleasant change of pace from all the sightseeing

artistic growth as he helped forge the new mannerist style.

🔄 GALLERIA DELL'ACCADEMIA

☎ 055 238 86 09; www.polomuseale .firenze.it; Via Ricasoli 60; €6.50; ⏰ 8.15am-6.50pm Tue-Sun

A lengthy queue marks the otherwise inauspicious entrance to this museum, built especially to hold a single masterpiece, Michelangelo's *David* (p14). The collection now also encompasses works by Botticelli and Taddeo Gaddi, a fine group of Russian icons, and several rooms of 14th-century paintings, including a remarkable embroidered *Coronazione della Vergine* (Coronation of the Virgin). However, it's *David* everyone's hot for – and for good reason. The sub-

tle detail – the veins in his sinewy arms, the muscles that seem to ripple under his marble skin, the change in expression as you move around the statue – *is* impressive. Michelangelo was also the master behind the unfinished *San Matteo* (St Matthew; 1503) in the same hall and also the four *Prigioni* ('prisoners' or 'slaves'; 1530) who seem to be writhing and struggling to free themselves from the marble. There is talk of moving *David* once again (p90) but don't hold your breath.

🔄 GIARDINO DEI SEMPLICI

☎ 055 275 74 02; Via Pier Antonio Micheli 3; €4; ⏰ 9am-1pm Thu-Tue, until 5pm Sat

Founded in 1545 to furnish medicine to the Medici, these gardens make a nice retreat in a

WHO'S THAT BLOKE?

Name: David
Occupation: world's most famous sculpture
Vital statistics: 516cm tall, 19 tonnes of mediocre-quality, pearly-white marble from Carrara
Previous residences: Commissioned to Michelangelo in 1501 by the Opera del Duomo for the cathedral, but subsequently placed in front of the Palazzo Vecchio on Piazza della Signoria, where he stayed until 1873.
Favourite journeys: It took 40 men four days to transport the statue along specially laid rails from Michelangelo's workshop behind the cathedral to Piazza della Signoria in 1504. Its journey from the piazza to the Galleria dell'Accademia in 1873 took seven days.
Outstanding features: (a) His expression which, from the left profile, appears serene and boyish; from the right, concentrated, manly and highly charged in anticipation of the gargantuan Goliath he is about to slay (b) the sense of counterbalanced weight rippling through his body, from the tension in his right hip to the tautness of his left arm.
Why the small dick?: In classical art a large or even normal-sized packet was not deemed elegant.
And the big head and hands?: David was designed to stand up high on a cathedral buttress in the apse, from which his head and hand would have appeared in proportion.
Beauty treatments: Body scrub with hydrochloric acid (1843); clay and cellulose pulp 'mud pack', bath in distilled water (2004).
Occupational hazards: Over the centuries he's been struck by lightning, attacked by rioters and had his toes bashed with a lunatic's hammer. The two pale white lines visible on his lower left arm are the spot where his arm was broken during the 1527 revolt when the Medici were kicked out of Florence.

stretch of the city with very little green space. Today its greenhouse is fragrant with citrus blossoms, while outdoors its 2.3 hectares are devoted to medicinal plants, Tuscan spices, and wildflowers from the Apennines.

🄾 MUSEO ARCHEOLOGICO

☎ 055 235 750; www.firenzemusei.it; Piazza Santissima Annunziata 9; €4; 🕑 2-7pm Mon, 8.30am-7pm Tue & Thu, 8.30am-4pm Wed & Fri-Sun

Skip the middling collection of artefacts from around the ancient world, and head straight to the museum's Etruscan collection, gathered largely from the region around Florence. Poor labelling and clinical glass-front cabinets feel dustily Victorian, but the collection of statuary, ceramics and jewellery is excellent. Look out for the monstrous bronze *Chimera* – a part lion, part goat and part snake cast in bronze and considered one of the masterpieces of Etruscan art.

🄲 MUSEO/CHIESA DI SAN MARCO

☎ 055 238 86 08; www.firenzemusei
.it; Piazza San Marco 1; €4; ⏱ 8.15am-
1.50pm Tue-Thu, 8.15am-6pm Fri,
8.15am-7pm Sat, 8.15am-7pm 2nd & 4th
Sun & 1st, 3rd & 5th Mon of month
Endowed generously by Cosimo il Vecchio (p76), this former Dominican monastery was an important font of early Renaissance art thanks mostly to its most famous resident, Fra Angelico. The attention to perspective and realistic portrayal of nature have lead critics to call his *Deposizione di Cristo* (Deposition of Christ; 1432) one of the first true paintings of the Renaissance. Fra Angelico was commissioned to produce this painting only because the original painter died. The early-Renaissance architecture of Michelozzo, especially his Chiostro di Sant'Antonio (1440), is also impressive. However, it is the monks' cells that are most haunting. At the top of the stairs lies Fra Angelico's most famous work, the exquisitely pastoral *Annunciazione* (c 1440). A stroll around each of the cells reveals snippets of many more fine frescoes, most executed by Fra Angelico. You can also visit the three-room suite that Savonarola called home from 1489 (p86).

🄲 OPIFICIO DELLE PIETRE DURE

☎ 055 265 1357; www.opificiodelle
pietredure.it, in Italian; Via degli Alfani
78; ⏱ 8.15am-1.45pm Mon-Sat, until
7pm Thu
Founded in 1588 to support the Florentine art of *pietre dure* – mosaiclike inlays of marble and semiprecious stones – this charming little museum explains how the works are created and includes remarkable examples of the craft, from portraits and trompe l'oeil tabletops to panoramic landscapes.

Art imitates life outside the Museo di San Marco

NEIGHBOURHOODS

SAN MARCO

MOVING TO THE 'BURBS?

It seems *David* is just too good-looking for his own good. After more than a century in his current digs (see p87), there is talk of moving Michelangelo's masterpiece once more. In early 2008, a top city official told the press that the volume of tourists in central Florence is over-taxing the city's infrastructure and even threatening the monuments themselves because of the vibrations caused by rumbling traffic. The official proposed moving *David* to the newly revitalised area around ex-Stazione Leopolda (p71). The city's mayor confirmed the fact that the plan was on the table, though said it was not yet a high priority and nothing had been decided. That likely means *David*'s centre-city perch is safe for at least another decade or so in a city where even high-priority public works are not known for breakneck speed.

🏛 SPEDALE DEGLI INNOCENTI
☎ 055 249 17 08; www.istitutodeglinno centi.it; Piazza della Santissima Annunziata 12; adult/concession €4/2.50; ☽ 8.30am-7pm Mon-Sat, 8.30am-2pm Sun

Shortly after its founding in 1421, Brunelleschi designed the *loggia* for what was Europe's first orphan-age. His use of rounded arches and Roman capitals mark it as arguably the first building of the Renaissance, while Andrea della Robbia (1435–1525) added the distinctive terracotta medallions of infants in swaddling clothes. Subsequent architects turned the piazza outside into a marvel of order and quirky symmetry.

🍴 EAT

🍴 CAFFELLATTE
Vegetarian   €€
☎ 055 247 88 78; Via degli Alfani 39r; ☽ 10am-8pm Mon, 8am-midnight Tue-Sun;

With a bas-relief marble cow adorning its counter, this quirky, turn-of-the-20th-century milk shop has, since the 1980s, pio-neered vegetarian and organic cooking, from its veggies and dairy products to the namesake *caffè latte*. The soups are thick and bursting with flavour, and the scones with fresh cream are worthy of a Cotswald teashop.

🍴 CARABÈ *Gelato*
☎ 055 289 476; www.gelatocarabe.com; Via Ricasoli 60r; ☽ 10am-midnight, closed mid-Dec–mid-Jan

The almond *granita* at the Sicilian-style Carabé *gelateria* gets our vote for the most refresh-ing concoction on the planet. Produced with sizzling passion by Antonio and Loredana Lisciandro, the shop's gelati and *sorbetti* are top quality, perhaps best enjoyed in the form of a *brioche* (a Sicilian ice-cream sandwich).

🍴 IL PIZZICAGNOLO
Classic Tuscan €

Via degli Alfani 5r; ⏰ **8am-3pm Mon-Sat, closed Aug**

An extremely jolly husband-and-wife team cook up simple but delicious Tuscan home cooking – including pastas, grilled vegetables and grilled meats – for rambunctiously hungry students on small budgets. Grab your meal to go or take a seat at one of the half-dozen tables in the no-frills dining annexe.

🍴 OIL SHOPPE
Quick Eats €

☎ **055 200 10 92; www.oleum.it; Via Sant'Egidio 22r;** ⏰ **11am-6pm Mon-Fri**

An institution among expat American students whose dollars aren't stretching like they used to, the meal-sized hot and cold sandwiches at this deli are delicious and priced to please. Fresh bread is packed with a filling quantity of ingredients that most places would eschew as un-Tuscan, but the results are fine by us.

🍴 OLIANDOLO
Classic Tuscan €€

☎ **055 211 296; Via Ricasoli 38r;** ⏰ **8am-10pm Mon-Sat**

For an unknown reason, tourists tend to overlook this simple but attractive eatery, which sits strategically between the Duomo and the Galleria dell'Accademia.

Prices are fair and geared to local office workers, while dishes run from creative salads and simple pastas to grilled meats with roast potatoes. Take your meal in the brightly whitewashed interior or angle for a table on the little sidewalk terrace.

🍴 RUTH'S
Vegetarian €€

☎ **055 248 08 88; www.kosheruth.com; Via Luigi Carlo Farini 2a;** ⏰ **lunch & dinner Sun-Thu, lunch Fri, dinner Sat;** Ⓥ

In the shade of the city's copper-domed synagogue, Ruth's offers a menu that is both largely vegetarian and strictly kosher. Try the fish couscous or felafel, and admire the pictures of Woody Allen and the Holy Land adorning the walls.

🍸 DRINK

🍸 LA MESCITA
Wine Bar

Via degli Alfani 70r; ⏰ **10.30am-4pm Mon-Sat, closed Aug**

Part *enoteca* (p15) and part bargain luncheonette, this unapologetically old-fashioned eatery serves up Tuscan specialties such as *trippa* (tripe) and *minestrone di verdura* (bean and vegetable soup). Noon-time tipplers and all-day drunks mix at the old marble-top bar, where you'll find good little *pannini* and *crostini* to go with the daily pourings of Chianti.

▼ LA ROBIGLIO *Cafe*
☎ 055 212 784; Via dei Servi 112r;
⏰ 7.30am-8pm

Known for its sweets and sublimely rich hot chocolate, this traditional *caffè* has a comfortably old-fashioned bourgeois air about it. The hot, sit-down meals aren't great value, but the sandwiches and baked goods make for a great pit stop between the Duomo and the Accademia. For a rarer treat, try the homemade candied roses and violets.

▼ REX CAFFÈ *Bar*
☎ 055 248 03 31; www.rexcafe.it; Via Fiesolana 23r; ⏰ 6pm-3am Sep-May

Long a fixture of Florence's nightlife, Rex still remains ahead of the curve. DJs spin electronica that generally remains soft enough for the trendy, young crowd to engage in conversation. The decor is classy kitsch, mixing cracked pottery mosaics (think Gaudí), low but warm lighting from wrought-iron fixtures, and a back room done up in blood red.

☆ PLAY

☆ BE BOP MUSIC CLUB
Live Music
☎ 055 21 97 99; Via dei Servi 76r;
⏰ 8pm-2am Mon-Sat

Inspired by the Swinging Sixties, this beloved retro bar and live-music venue features everything from Led Zeppelin and Beatles

The colourful Rex Caffè silently awaits its chatty young clientele

cover bands to swing jazz, soul and 1970s funk.

⭐ JAZZ CLUB *Live Music*
☎ 055 247 97 00; www.jazzclub firenze.com; Via Nuova de' Caccini 3; compulsory 12-month membership €6; ⏰ 9pm-1am Tue-Sat

Florence's top jazz venue hosts quality acts, both local and from wider afield, in an atmospheric vaulted basement. Besides jazz,

you can catch salsa, blues, Dixieland, and world-music acts.

⭐ TEATRO DELLA PERGOLA *Theatre/Classical Music*
☎ 055 226 4353; www.pergola.firenze .it, in Italian; Via della Pergola 18

Built in the 1650s, this wonderful little baroque theatre is the ideal venue for chamber music. It also stages classic plays from Shakespeare to Pirandello.

>SANTA CROCE ✓

The largest of Florence's historic quarters, Santa Croce takes its name from the sprawling Franciscan monastery (p96) that anchors the neighbourhood. It possesses such a density of masterpieces that it's said sensitive souls can grow dizzy and confused – even hallucinate – as they succumb to Stendhal's syndrome (p97), named for the French novelist who first described the phenomenon. If Santa Croce doesn't have you swooning, try the medieval Palazzo (now Museo) del Bargello (p97), which possesses the world's greatest collection of Renaissance sculpture. Still not flinching? The food might just test your nerves. Santa Croce is the city's unofficial gourmet ghetto, with celestial addresses such as Cibrèo (p103) and Enoteca Pinchiorri (p102) as well as plenty of more earthbound options. If you're still on your feet at midnight, the carnival-like crowds that swell the bars and clubs around Via de' Benci will give you a final run for your money.

SANTA CROCE

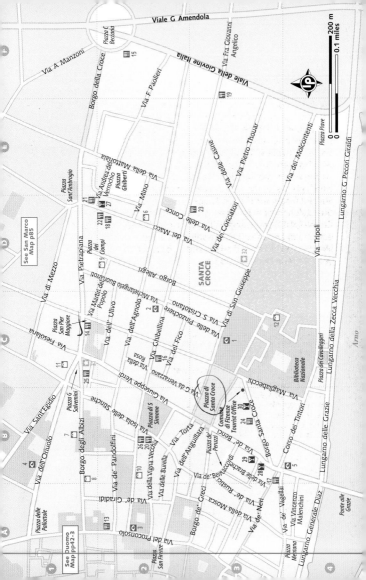

Viale G Amendola

Piazza G
Beccaria

Via A Manzoni

Borgo della Croce

Via F Paoletti

Via della Giovine Italia

Via Fra Giovanni
Angelico

15

19

Via delle Casine

Via Pietro Thouar

Via dei Malcontenti

Piazza Piave

Lungarno G Pecori Giraldi

See San Marco
Map p85

Piazza
Sant'Ambrogio

Via Andrea del Verrocchio

Via della Mattonaia

Piazza
Ghiberti

Via Mino

21

27

22 18

6

Via del Macci

Via delle Conce

Via dei Conciatori

23

Via Tripoli

Via di Mezzo

Via Pietrapiana

Piazza
dei
Ciompi

9

Borgo Allegri

SANTA
CROCE

30

Via di S. Giuseppe

Via Fiesolana

Piazza
San Pier
Maggiore

Via Martiri del
Popolo

Via dell'Ulivo

Via dell'Agnolo

Via Michelangelo Buonarroti

Via delle Pinzochere

Via S. Cristofano

14

2

25

Via della
Rosa

Via Ghibellina

Via del Fico

16

1

12

Biblioteca
Nazionale

Piazza dei Cavalleggeri

Lungarno della Zecca Vecchia

Arno

Via Sant'Egidio

Via dell'Oriuolo

Piazza G
Salvemini

11

4

Borgo degli Albizi

Via della Isola delle Stinche

Via Giuseppe Verdi

Via G. da Verrazzano

Piazza di
Santa Croce

Via de' Pepi

Via Magliabechi

Piazza di S
Simone

26 20

10

Piazza de'
Peruzzi

Comune
di Firenze
Tourist Office

24 30

Borgo Santa Croce

Corso dei Tintori

Lungarno delle Grazie

See
Duomo
Map pp42-3

Piazza
delle
Pallottole

Via de' Giraldi

Via de' Pandolfini

Borgo de' Greci

Via della Vigna Vecchia

Via delle Burella

7

8

13

Via del Proconsolo

Piazza
San Firenze

Via Torta

Via dell'Anguillara

Via de' Benci

Via de' Rustici

Via de' Bentaccordi

Via de' Neri

Via della Mosca

Via de' Vagellai

Via Vincenzo Malenchini

Lungarno Generale Diaz

29

28

5

Piazza
Mentana

Ponte alle
Grazie

200 m
0.1 miles

200
0

SEE

BASILICA DI SANTA CROCE

☎ 055 246 61 05; Piazza di Santa Croce; €5 incl Museo dell'Opera; ⏱ 9.30am-5.30pm Mon-Sat, 1-5.30pm Sun

Behind an opulent candy-coloured facade (actually a 19th-century neo-Gothic addition), the nave of this Gothic church, built between 1294 and 1385, is surprisingly austere. EM Forster described the interior as 'barn-like', because of the timber, A-frame–style ceiling and general lac- of finery. But lurking in the transept is a series of chapels brightly decked out with masterly fresco cycles. Unfortunately, only parts of Giot-to's cycle depicting the life of St Francis survive. Those by his loyal pupil Taddeo Gaddi are in much better shape, as are Taddi's *Last Supper* in the refectory – considered his masterpiece – and his *Crucifixion* in the sacristy. The basilica church also serves as a kind of Florentine pantheon, including the tombs of Michelangelo, sculpted by Giorgio Vasari, Galileo Galilei and an empty monument to Dante (who is buried in Ravenna, where he died in exile). Don't miss Brunelleschi's Cappella de' Pazzi in the cloister to the right of the church. Its geometric harmony and exquisite terracotta medallions of the apos-

Hansel and Gretel would be at home in the Piazza di Santa Croce

GOING WEAK AT THE KNEES

'I reached the point where one encounters celestial sensations,' wrote Stendhal upon his 1817 visit to Florence. 'On leaving Santa Croce, I felt a pulsating in my heart. Life was draining out of me, and I feared I'd fall as I walked.'

Stendhal is not the only visitor to Florence who has suffered in this way. In her 1989 book entitled *Stendhal's Syndrome*, Italian psychologist Graziella Magherini documents dozens of similar cases during several decades working at a Florence hospital.

According to Magherini, symptoms of Stendhal's syndrome can range from dizziness and physical weakness to fainting and even hallucinations. Of course, the heat of Florentine summers, when combined with a day of walking and insufficient fluid intake, can lead to similar effects. But in her book, Magherini maintains that certain sensitive souls reawaken past traumas when confronted by the ego-dissolving density of art in a place such as Florence.

Think you might be susceptible? Between your bouts with the city's masterpieces, we recommend eating properly, staying hydrated, and ensuring sufficient rest for mind and body.

tles by Luca della Robbia make it one of the great achievements of Renaissance architecture. Finally the church's small museum harbours a *Crucifixion* by Cimabue, Donatello's gilded bronze statue *St Louis of Toulouse* (1424), and frescoes by Giotto, including an *Ultima Cena* (Last Supper; 1333).

◉ MUSEO CASA BUONARROTI
☎ 055 241 752; www.casabuonarroti.it; Via Ghibellina 70; €6.50; ⏰ 9.30am-2pm Wed-Mon

Though Michelangelo never lived in Casa Buonarroti, his heirs devoted some of the artist's hard-earned wealth to the construction of this 17th-century palazzo to honour his memory. The little museum contains frescoes of the artist's life and two of his most important early works – the serene, bas-relief

Madonna of the Stairs and the unfinished *Battle of the Centaurs*.

◉ MUSEO DEL BARGELLO
☎ 055 238 86 06; Via del Proconsolo 4; €7; ⏰ 8.15am-6pm Tue-Sat, 2nd & 4th Sun & 1st, 3rd & 5th Mon of the month

Crowds clamour to see *David*, but few rush to Michelangelo's early works in the Bargello. The artist was just 22 when a cardinal commissioned him to create the drunken *Bacchus* displayed in the ground-floor hall. His large roundel of the Madonna and Child with the infant St John, known as *Tondo Pitti*, portrays the halo-bare pair in a very human light. However, the collection's most illustrious member is another *David*. Donatello's bronze version from the 1440s, the first freestanding nude to be sculpted since classical times, is

Rebecca Gill
Architectural historian, British Institute of Florence

Even after two years in Florence, Rebecca Gill says she's constantly discovering something new, even if it's just the way a familiar building reveals itself at different times of year, or under a different light. According to Gill, no other Italian city possesses Florence's sheer density of outstanding art and architecture. Ironically, the city was preserved by the stagnation following its Renaissance flowering – no money to tear down the old and make way for the new. 'This has also endowed the place with a stylistic aesthetic coherence that's integral to its beauty,' she says. 'And yet, Florence is small, so it has an intimacy that other cities just don't have. You feel that you can really begin to know it in, say, five days.' **Her favourite building:** the Cappella de' Pazzi in the Basilica di Santa Croce (p96). Why? 'Because of its precision, and because it sums up Brunelleschi's development as an architect.'

elegant and slenderly androgynous – a curious contrast from Michelangelo's he-man version. These are just a few highlights of an extraordinary collection that includes works by Bandinelli, Cellini, Danti, Giambologna and Verrocchio, as well as a large group of terracotta pieces by the prolific della Robbia family. And don't neglect the Palazzo del Bargello itself, which served as the republic's high court for three centuries, and then as a Medici prison. Built in the 1250s, it's a smaller and purer version of Italian Gothic than the oft-renovated Palazzo Vecchio.

MUSEO DI FIRENZE COM'ERA

☎ 055 261 65 45; Via dell'Oriuolo 24; €2.70; ⏰ 9am-1.30pm Mon-Tue, 9am-6.30pm Sat

Tucked behind Brunelleschi's dome, this melancholic little museum tells the story of Florence through a series of paintings from the Renaissance through to the 19th century. A newer annexe also displays prehistoric, Etruscan and Roman artefacts, including a diorama of the city as it looked in Roman times.

MUSEO HORNE

☎ 055 244 661; www.museohorne.it, in Italian; Via de' Benci 6; €5; ⏰ 9am-1pm Mon-Sat

One of the many eccentric Brits who made Florence home in the early 20th century, Herbert Percy Horne bought and renovated this Renaissance palazzo, then installed his eclectic collection of 14th- and 15th-century Italian art, ceramics, furniture and other oddments. There are a few works by masters such as Giotto and Filippo Lippi. More interesting is the furniture, some of it exquisite.

SHOP

LA BOTTEGA DEL CIOCCOLATO Food

☎ 055 200 1609; www.bottegadelcioccolato.it; Via del Macci 50; ⏰ closed Aug

Andrea Bianchini makes his prize-winning chocolate on the premises of his chic little side-street shop. Unafraid to experiment, he marries the finest chocolates with flavours such as mango with coriander and ginger, lemon with violet, rosemary with sea salt, and passionfruit with Szechuan pepper.

MAESTRI DI FABBRICA Crafts

☎ 055 242 321; www.maestridifabbrica.it; Borgo degli Albizi 68r; ⏰ 10am-8pm

Ranged over four large rooms in the Renaissance Palazzo Albizzi, this high-end factory outlet offers up some of the most stylish goods available from Tuscan artisans, from blown glass and alabaster to sleek contemporary furnishings.

MARCHI *Crafts*

☎ 055 234 0415; Borgo degli Albizi 69r
Need a break from Tuscan? This shop offers a beautiful selection of objects from Asia and Africa, ranging from Senegalese masks to Thai silks. The wares may be imported, but the pair of sisters who run the shop select their merchandise with a distinctly Italian flair.

MERCATO DEI PULCI
Antiques

Piazza dei Ciompi; ⏰ 10am-1pm, 4-7pm Mon-Sat
While prices are much higher than the name implies (*mercato dei pulci* means flea market), this outdoor market is nevertheless still worth a gander for patient pickers game to bring home a piece of Old Tuscany.

MONASTICA *Crafts*

☎ 055 211 006; Via Ghibellina 127r
Who knew the monastic life could be so sensual? This quaint shop run by nuns from the nearby Badia Fiorentina offers up divine soaps, perfumes, jams and jellies and other all-natural gifts produced in monasteries around Italy.

SBIGOLI TERRECOTTE
Ceramics

☎ 055 247 97 13; www.sbigoli terrecotte.it; Via Sant'Egidio 4r
This family-owned operation churns out beautiful ceramics in the combination of rusticity and refinement that marks the classic Florence style. The shop has shelves and shelves of the stuff, while in back lies the workshop where the Sbigoli family produce their craft and also offer hands-on workshops for budding potters.

SCUOLA DEL CUOIO *Leather*

☎ 055 244 533; www.scuoladelcuoio .com; Via San Giuseppe 5r; ⏰ 10am-6pm
Hidden in a courtyard behind Santa Croce, this store and workshop features a long corridor where craftsmen stand at their stations fashioning their leathergoods by hand. You can buy the high-quality wares at prices somewhat more reasonable than at most shops, though don't expect bargains.

🍴 EAT

🍴 ALLE MURATE
Contemporary Tuscan €€€€

☎ 055 240 618; Via del Proconsolo 16r;
⏰ dinner Tue-Sun
Set under the vaulted ceilings of a medieval palazzo, your feast begins with the art on the walls, including the earliest known portraits of Dante and Boccaccio. Then there's the food – a contemporary take on Tuscan cuisine with a feisty southern Italian kick, such as the sea bass in ginger sauce and buttery salt cod with spinach. Chefs beaver away

behind glass, and remnants of Roman Florence lurk in the cellar. Wine – an insatiable passion of charismatic owner Umberto Montan – is yet another draw.

ANTICO NOÈ
Classic Tuscan €€
☎ 055 234 08 38; Volta di San Piero 6r; meals €30; ⏰ noon-midnight Mon-Sat
Hidden down a covered medieval alley, this trattoria occupies an old butcher's shop that still boasts white marble-clad walls and wrought-iron meat hooks. The menu is filled with down-to-earth

Tuscan fodder. For a quick bite, the adjacent shop delivers juicy panini made from spit-roasted meat. The roast pork with garlicky sautéed spinach comes highly recommended.

DOLCI & DOLCEZZA
Bakery
☎ 055 234 54 58; Piazza C Beccaria 8r; ⏰ 8.30am-7.30pm Tue-Sat, 9am-1pm Sun, closed Aug
Done up in mint-green panelling like an aristocratic boudoir, this sweet little bakery is considered to be one of the city's best. The

Delicious anticipation at the bar of Trattoria I Fratellini (p104)

NEIGHBOURHOODS

SANTA CROCE

remarkable flourless chocolate cake is worth the walk to the old city's western edge. The little espresso bar is also first-rate.

❤️ ENOTECA PINCHIORRI
Classic Tuscan €€€€
☎ 055 242 757; www.enotecapinchiorri .com; Via Ghibellina 87r; 🕐 **dinner Tue-Wed, lunch & dinner Thu-Sat, closed Aug**
This temple to fine food and wine invariably ranks as Florence's top restaurant. Set in a 16th-century palazzo, the atmosphere is surprisingly easy-going despite the pink-toned finery and gilt-framed art. The wine list is extensive – among the best in Italy. Dress well (men should wear jackets), bring plenty of plastic (expect to pay upwards of €200 per person) and reserve far in advance for an unforgettable evening.

❤️ GASTRONOMIA GIULIANO
Classic Tuscan €
☎ 055 287 380; Via de' Neri 5r; 🕐 **7am-2pm, 5-8pm Mon-Fri, 7am-2pm Sat, closed Aug**
One of the best of the city's *rosticerrie* (caterers selling prepared dishes to go), the gracious Giuliano proudly serves up grilled meats, hot and cold pasta dishes and grilled and sautéed vegetables as well as a range of sandwich fixings. It's the ideal place to stock up on picnic fare.

❤️ IL PIZZAIUOLO *Pizza* €€
☎ 055 241 171; Via dei Macci 113r; 🕐 **lunch & dinner Mon-Sat, closed Aug**
Despite a historic preference for thinner crusts, Neapolitans with their thick crusts have come to dominate the Florentine pizza scene. With its wood-burning oven and perfectly matured dough, this simple Neapolitan-run joint is among the best. Be prepared to queue at nights and weekends.

❤️ ORA D'ARIA
Contemporary Tuscan €€€€
☎ 055 200 16 99; www.oradaria ristorante.com; Via Ghibellina 3Cr; 🕐 **dinner Mon-Sat, closed Aug**
An empty birdcage greets you as you enter this stylishly minimalist gallery. It's a subtle joke – the restaurant is named after that precious hour in the day when inmates cooped up in the city prison opposite (shut in the 1980s) were allowed to walk about the central court. Chef and rising star Marco Stabile helps you free your palate with dishes such as pigeon-stuffed *tortelli* with foie gras in a pecorino (cheese made from sheep's milk) cream sauce, steak tartar with raw asparagus and fried garlic, or warm hen and spider-crab salad with artichoke puree and vanilla-scented oil.

🍴 OSTERIA DEL CAFFÈ ITALIANO *Classic Tuscan* €€€

☎ 055 289 368; Via Isola delle Stinche 11r; ⏱ lunch & dinner Tue-Sun, closed Jan

From the man who brought you Alle Murate (p100), Umberto Montano's more modest address offers not just good value but also perfectly prepared dishes such as *bistecca alla fiorentina* (€50 per kg), served with beans, greens and roast spuds. The setting is quaintly old-fashioned, with its gleaming wooden antiques and glowing lamps. The restaurant's adjacent pizzeria is dead simple, with just three choices available, a few tables and only the finest ingredients. Arrive early if you want to sit – otherwise get your pizza to go and enjoy it on nearby Piazza di Santa Croce.

🍴 RISTORANTE CIBRÈO *Classic Tuscan* €€€€

☎ 055 234 11 00; Via Andrea del Verrocchio 8r; ⏱ 12.50-2.30pm & 7-11.15pm Tue-Sat, closed Aug

At his flagship restaurant, Fabio Picchi (below) sticks largely to ancient and often humble Florentine recipes, such as *salsicce di maiale con fagioli e cavolo nero* (sausage with beans and greens) and a kind of pudding of ricotta and potatoes adorned with meat sauce and parmesan. Finish your meal with a divine cheesecake dressed with bitter orange marmalade. Reserve as far in advance as possible. If you're on a budget or couldn't finagle a reservation, you join the queue (reservations not accepted) for the same dishes from the same kitchen at virtually half the price at Cibrèino, the significantly more hectic trattoria that sits next door.

PICCHI, PICCHI

'The Florentine is stingy by nature, yet obsessed with quality', Fabio Picchi once declared. 'There is a constant tension between frugality and the noble predilection for the best.' So when in 2004 Wine Spectator called him the world's master of that humblest ingredient – tripe – Picchi regarded the compliment the highest he could hope for.

Picchi opened Ristorante Cibrèo (above) in 1979, and soon won the hearts of the world's foodies. Legendary critic Patricia Wells called his restaurant one of her 10 favourites in the world. Though known for his theatrical personality, Picchi's cooking is renowned not for fireworks but the careful balancing act between richness and restraint – and of course the uncompromising search for the best ingredients.

Today, his little empire, which is clustered around Piazza Sant'Ambrogio, has expanded to include the adjacent trattoria Cibrèino (above) and tiny, super refined Caffè Cibrèo (p105). Finally, Teatro del Sale (p104) combines a highly regarded buffet with dinner theatre.

Vivoli is just one of a host of suberb *gelaterias*

🍴 TEATRO DEL SALE
Contemporary Tuscan   €€€
☎ 055 200 14 92; www.teatrodelsale
.com; Via dei Macci 111r; 🕙 9-11am,
12.30-2.30pm & 7.30-11pm Tue-Sat,
closed Aug

For both value for money and fine
entertainment, this old Florentine
theatre steals the show. Join the
club (annual membership €5) and
make yourself at home in a leather armchair between bookshelves
in the cosy wood-panelled library
or in a director's chair around
fold-up tables in the airy theatre
space. Wait for the chef to yell
out what's cooking through the

glass hatch – a buffet of antipasti,
starters, mains, dessert and coffee.
Lunch is a laidback affair while
dinner is followed by an evening
of drama, music or comedy (advance reservations are required)
arranged by artistic director
Maria Cassi, a famous Florentine
actress and the wife of Fabio
Picchi.

🍴 TRATTORIA I FRATELLINI
Classic Tuscan   €
☎ 055 234 73 89; Via Ghibellina 27r;
🕙 8am-5pm

Amid all the high-flying dining
in Santa Croce, this combination
grocery shop, wine bar and trattoria seems to have changed little
since it opened in the 1950s. Even
prices remain stuck in time. Two
courses (perhaps minestrone followed by rotisserie chicken) and
a glass of quaffable Chianti cost
under €10. And you won't regret
the calories in the homemade
tiramisu.

🍴 VALLE DEI CEDRI
Middle Eastern   €€
☎ 055 234 63 04; Borgo Santa Croce 11r;
🕙 lunch & dinner Mon-Sat

This new offering just off Piazza
di Santa Croce offers up first-rate
Lebanese fare made from fresh
Tuscan ingredients. The *maza*
platter includes a range of classic
dishes such as baba ghanoosh

and felafel, while the meats and kebabs are grilled to succulence.

¶¶ VESTRI *Gelato*
☎ 055 234 03 74; www.vestri.it; Borgo degli Albizi 11r; ⏲ 10.30am-8pm Mon-Sat

Inside his little shop, Leonardo Vestri brews up what is the most decadent hot chocolate in the city. It also comes in an equally delicious chilled version during summer months. Leonardo also makes top-notch chocolate-flavoured gelati, including chocolate and Sicilian oranges and a zinging combination of dark chocolate and hot peppers.

¶¶ VIVOLI *Gelato*
☎ 055 292 334; Via Isola delle Stinche 7; ⏲ 9am-1am Tue-Sat

A long-time favourite of Florentine families on their afternoon constitutional, Vivoli still deserves praise for its fine gelati, especially its perfectly balanced mixtures of chocolate with flavours such as cinnamon, hazelnut and orange.

DRINK

When in doubt about your evening, join the crowds along Via de' Benci where, on warm nights, crowds spill out from the bars and clubs into the streets. The steps of Santa Croce attracts students

with their bottles of plonk and can also make for an evening's entertainment.

⥾ CAFFÈ CIBRÈO *Cafe*
☎ 055 234 58 53; Via Andrea del Verrocchio 5r; ⏲ 8am-1pm Tue-Sat, closed Aug

Just across from the restaurant of the same name, Fabio Picchi's (p103) super-refined cafe serves excellent espresso and sweets as well as light meals. The *passata di peperoni gialli* (yellow bell-pepper soup) is thrilling. Choose between shady terrace seating or the cosy, clubby interior with its red-velvet chairs and coffered wood ceiling.

CALCIO STORICO
Greco-Roman rite? Colourful Renaissance pageant? Controlled hooliganism? Actually *calcio storico* (historic soccer) is all of the above. A combination of boxing, wrestling, rugby and soccer, the game pits 27 very burly men in brightly coloured costumes. They beat each other bloody (literally) as they try to move the ball up and down the field – or in this case, Piazza di Santa Croce, which is transformed into a giant sandpit. The lead-up to the game includes a 500-strong parade of men in Renaissance garb. By tradition, two preliminary matches occur at the beginning of June, with the finale during the Festa di San Giovanni (June 24).

There is always a ready supply of Chianti wine somewhere nearby in Florence

☿ LOCH NESS Bar
☎ 055 200 10 57; Via de' Benci 19r;
🕐 8pm-3am

The tagline of this bar-club is 'Get messy with Nessie', and if you're determined to get pissed without having to use a word of Italian, this is your place. Painted the colour of a London telephone box, it offers up foozeball, live acoustic music Tuesday and Saturday, two-for-ones until 11pm every day, and loads of eager Anglophone punters.

☿ MOYO Bar
☎ 055 247 97 38; www.moyo.it; Via de' Benci 23r; 🕐 8pm-2am Sun-Thu, until 3am Fri & Sat

The anchor of the Via de' Benci bar scene, Moyo boasts a cavernous, almost industrial interior softened by a choice assortment of candelabras and chandeliers. The first venue in Florence to offer wi-fi, it also delivers a generous *aperitivo* buffet to hungry hipsters.

☿ PICCOLO CAFFÈ Bar
☎ 055 200 10 57; Borgo Santa Croce 23r; 🕐 6.30pm-2am

Looking vaguely like a '50s-style diner, Piccolo is the place where gay Florence begins its night. The vibe is relaxed, there is more conversation than cruising, and weather permitting, the crowd spills out into the outdoor smoking section (ie the street).

NEIGHBOURHOODS

SANTA CROCE

PLAY
⭐ TWICE *Nightclub*
☎ 055 247 63 56; www.twiceclub.com; Via Giuseppe Verdi 57r; ⏰ 7pm-2pm, until 4pm Wed-Sat

Mainstream fun is on tap at this venue that starts the night as a wine bar and then turns into a dance club after 11pm (hence the name). The clientele tends to be Pretty Young Things in search of same. After the *aperitivo* buffet closes down, the DJs start to arrive with their iPods stuffed with hip-hop and Top 40 dance hits.

⭐ Y@G *Nightclub*
☎ 055 246 9022; www.yagbar.com; Via dei Macci 8r; ⏰ 6pm-3am Sep-May

The mainstream answer to Tabasco (p57), this relaxed gay club caters to a younger crowd of both sexes with its large bar, small dance floor offering up Diva dance hits on the flat-screen, and a separate lounge done up in wallpaper of a clever plaid.

>BOBOLI & SAN MINIATO AL MONTE

It's remarkable how swiftly you can beat your retreat from the congested pavements of central Florence. Just south of the Arno, sylvan scenes reach down almost to the city's centre, and the sprawling elegance of the Boboli gardens (p112), built for the pleasure of Medici princes, is only the beginning. The smaller, more steeply pitched and better manicured Bardini gardens (opposite) proffer stunning city views. Just a little further and suddenly you're in a network of country lanes and tree-lined avenues. Wind your way past hillside orchards hidden discreetly by ancient stone walls as you make your way east towards San Miniato al Monte (opposite). This 11th-century Romanesque church is one of the city's oldest, and rivalled only by the Duomo for its beauty. After surveying its panoramic views, head back down to the banks of the Arno, where some of the city's choicest nightlife awaits you.

BOBOLI & SAN MINIATO AL MONTE

◉ SEE
Chiesa di San Miniato
  al Monte 1 G5
Chiesa di Santa Felicità... 2 D2
Forte di Belvedere........... 3 D4
Galleria Palatina..........(see 9)
Giardino Bardini............. 4 E3
Giardino Bardini –
  Main Entrance............. 5 D3
Giardino di Boboli 6 C3
Museo delle Porcellane... 7 D4
Museo Zoologico La
  Specola........................ 8 B3
Palazzo Pitti 9 C3

Porta San Niccolò 10 F3
Villa Bardini.................11 D3

◻ SHOP
Madova........................12 D2

❚❙ EAT
Antica Mescita
  San Niccolò................13 F3
Da Ruggero...................14 A6
I Tarocchi 15 E3
La Mangiatoia 16 B3

▾ DRINK
Caffè La Torre...............17 G3
Enoteca Fuori Porta......18 F3
James Joyce..................19 H3
Le Volpi e l'Uva............20 D2
Negroni 21 E3
Plasma.........................22 H3
Zoe..............................23 E3

★ PLAY
Montecarla Club...........24 E3

Please see over for map

SEE

CHIESA DI SAN MINIATO AL MONTE

☎ 234 27 31; Via Monte alle Croci; admission free; ⏱ 8am-noon & 3-6pm Mon-Thu & Sat, 3-6pm Fri & Sun Nov-Apr, 8am-7pm May-Oct

Miniato was an early Christian martyr who, after his beheading in central Florence, walked up to this hillside spot with his severed head tucked under his arm. It's easy to see why he chose this as his final resting place – the views across Florence are spectacular. So is the church itself. Begun in the early 11th century, it's a marvel of Tuscan Romanesque with its geometric marble facade, Byzantine-style mosaics, floors paved in beautiful patterns, and duplex-style choir raised above an even older and more atmospheric crypt. The church also has frescoes by Agnolo Gaddi, terracotta sculpture by Luca della Robbia, and a free-standing chapel by Michelozzo. Come around 4.30pm (in winter) or 5.30pm (summer) and you may hear the monks' Gregorian chant wafting up from the crypt. Bus 13 from Santa Maria Novella station stops nearby.

CHIESA DI SANTA FELICITÀ

Piazza Santa Felicità; ⏱ 9am-noon & 3.30-6pm Mon-Sat, noon-1pm Sun

Possibly founded by Syrian merchants as early as the 2nd century, the current church is largely a Renaissance construction. Its most extraordinary feature is Brunelleschi's small Cappella Barbadori, which is adorned by frescoes by Jacopo Pontormo (1494–1557) of the Annunciation and a Deposition from the Cross, in garish reds, pinks and oranges. Note also that the Corridoio Vasariano (p48) passes right across the facade so the Medici could hear Mass like any good Christians, but without having to mix with the common folk.

FORTE DI BELVEDERE

☎ 055 23 320; Costa San Giorgio; ⏱ 9am-sunset

Sitting on a promontory above the Giardino di Boboli, this fort was designed by Bernardo Buontalenti to guard the Medici family treasury. Its grassy ramparts provide stunning views across Florence as well as the villas and orchards south of the Arno. Inside the simple but stately main building are occasional contemporary art exhibitions (admission €5).

GIARDINO DI BARDINI

☎ 055 238 85; Costa San Giorgio 4-6 & Via de' Bardi 1r; €6 incl Boboli entrance; ⏱ 8.15am-7.30pm Jun-Aug, 8.15am-6.30pm Apr-May & Sep-Oct, 8.15am-5.30pm Mar, 8.15am-4.30pm Nov-Feb

Smaller and better manicured than the adjacent Giardino di Boboli,

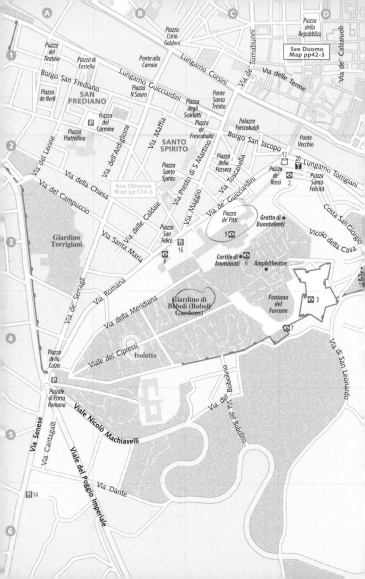

A1 Piazza del Tiratoio
A1 Piazza di Cestello
A1 Piazza de' Nerli
A1 Borgo San Frediano
A1 SAN FREDIANO
A2 Piazza Piattellina
A2 Piazza del Carmine
A2 Via dell'Ardiglione
A2 Via del Leone
A2 Via della Chiesa
A2 Via del Campuccio
A3 Giardino Torrigiani
A3 Via Santa Maria
A3 Via de' Serragli
A4 Via Romana
A4 Piazza della Calza
A5 Piazzale di Porta Romana
A5 Via Senese
A5 Via Cantagalli
A5 Viale Nicolo Machiavelli
A5 Viale del poggio Imperiale
A6 Via Dante

B1 Piazza Carlo Goldoni
B1 Ponte alla Carraia
B1 Lungarno Guicciardini
B1 Piazza N Sauro
B2 Via Maffia
B2 SANTO SPIRITO
B2 Piazza Santo Spirito
B2 Via Presto di S Martino
B2 Via delle Caldaie
B3 Piazza San Felice
B3 Via Maggio
B3 Via della Meridiana
B4 Giardino di Boboli (Boboli Gardens)
B4 Viale dei Cipressi
B4 Isolotto

C1 Piazza Carlo Goldoni
C1 Lungarno Corsini
C1 Via de' Tornabuoni
C1 Via delle Terme
C1 Ponte Santa Trinita
C2 Piazza degli Scarlatti
C2 Palazzo Frescobaldi
C2 Piazza de' Frescobaldi
C2 Borgo San Jacopo
C2 Ponte Vecchio
C2 Piazza della Passera
C2 Via Toscanella
C2 Piazza de' Rossi
C2 Lungarno Torrigiani
C2 Piazza Santa Felicita
C3 Piazza de' Pitti
C3 Grotto di Buontalenti
C3 Via de' Guicciardini
C3 Cortile di Ammanati
C3 Amphitheatre
C3 Fontana del Forcone
C3 Costa San Giorgio
C3 Vicolo della Cava
C4 Via del Bobolino
C4 Via del Boboli
C4 Via di San Leonardo

D1 Piazza della Repubblica
D1 See Duomo Map pp42-3
D1 Via de' Calzaiuoli

See Oltrarno Map pp124-5

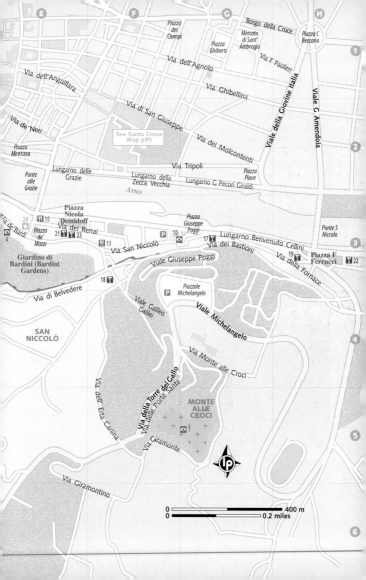

E

F

G

H

Piazza dei Ciompi

Piazza Ghiberti

Borgo della Croce

Mercato di Sant' Ambrogia

Piazza C Beccaria

1

Via dell'Anguillara

Via dell'Agnolo

Via F Paolieri

Via Ghibellina

Via de' Neri

Via di San Giuseppe

Via dei Molcontenti

Viale della Giovine Italia

Viale G Amendola

See Santa Croce Map p95

Piazza Mentana

Lungarno delle Grazie

Via Tripoli

Piazza Piave

2

Ponte alle Grazie

Lungarno della Zecca Vecchia

Lungarno G Pecori Giraldi

Arno

Piazza Nicola Demidoff

Piazza Giuseppe Poggi

Ponte S Niccolo

Via de' Bardi

24 ▮ 15

Piazza de' Mozzi

21 ▮ 23

Via dei Renai

13 ▮

Lungarno Benvenuto Cellini

17 ▮

Via dei Bastioni

19 ▮

Piazza F Ferrucci

▮ 22

3

4

P 10

Via della Fornace

P

Via San Niccolò

Giardino di Bardini (Bardini Gardens)

18 ▮

Viale Giuseppe Poggi

Piazzale Michelangelo

Via di Belvedere

P Piazzale Michelangelo

Viale Galileo Galilei

Viale Michelangelo

4

SAN NICCOLÒ

Via dell' Erta Canina

Via della Torre del Gallo

Via delle Porte Sante

Via Monte alle Croci

MONTE ALLE CROCI

5

Via Giramonte

Via Giramontino

⊕ LP

0   400 m
0   0.2 miles

6

these steeply pitched gardens spill down the hillside almost to the Arno. Views across the Florentine rooftops are some of the city's loveliest, made all the more so for the gardens' grottoes, fountains, classical statuary, and monumental baroque staircase. A springtime stroll is especially rewarding when by turns azaleas, peonies, wisteria and irises come into bloom. Escape sun, rain or heat under the *loggia* (covered area on the side of a building), which also doubles as a cafe.

🌀 GIARDINO DI BOBOLI

☎ 055 238 85; www.polomuseale .firenze.it/english/musei/boboli /default.asp; Piazza de' Pitti; €6 incl

Giardino di Bardini; 🕙 **8.15am-7.30pm Jun-Aug, 8.15am-6.30pm Apr-May & Sep-Oct, 8.15am-5.30pm Mar, 8.15am-4.30pm Nov-Feb**

Despite the volumes of visitors and a slightly shop-worn mien, the Boboli gardens (see also p18) remain both a marvel of Tuscan Renaissance landscape architecture and, in its further reaches, a fine escape from the tourist hordes. Perhaps its most impressive feature is the stately **Viale dei Cipressi**, a grand, cypress-lined avenue that leads down to **Isolotto**, a marvellous ornamental pond adorned with a marble Neptune and nymphs and, in warmer weather, fragrant citrus trees. Nearer the Palazzo Pitti, a

The slopes of the Giardino di Bardini offer beautiful views over Florence

GRAND TOTAL

Florence has long been a traveller staple. From the 17th to 19th centuries, the education of a British gentleman was not considered complete until he had embarked on a 'Grand Tour', with a mandatory stop in Florence for a crash course in Renaissance art.

With the advent of train travel, Florence became accessible to a widening class of travellers, including the upper-middle-class women of EM Forster's *A Room with a View*. In fact, the city attracted an enormous community of Anglo expats in the 19th and early 20th centuries, from poets Robert and Elizabeth Barrett Browning to eccentrics such as Herbert Percy Horne (p99).

Except during wartime, tourist numbers kept climbing throughout the 20th century, reaching somewhere between eight and 11 million annually in recent years. Tourism represents the largest share of the city's economy even if, according to tourist officials, the majority don't even spend the night.

The crowds can be discouraging. However, the vast majority frequent what has been dubbed the 'Golden Triangle', which extends from the Galleria dell'Accademia, past the Duomo and Piazza della Signoria, over the Ponte Vecchio to the Palazzo Pitti, then over to Santa Croce.

The good news is that just a few blocks outside the Golden Triangle, Florence reverts to something like a normal city. While you won't be the only tourist, the walk up to San Miniato (p119) provides beautiful breathing room. For more ideas on how to beat the crowds, see p34.

fleshy Venus by Giambologna rises from the waves in the **Grotta del Buontalenti**, a fanciful grotto designed by the eponymous artist. Don't miss the haunting 'face' sculpture (1998) by Polish sculptor Igor Mitoraj (b 1944), located near the top of the Viale dei Cipressi. It seems to grow out of the garden itself. And if you head straight uphill from the Palazzo Pitti, past a Renaissance **amphitheatre** and menagerie of ancient Roman and baroque sculpture, you eventually reach the **Museo delle Porcellane** (admission included), home to the Sèvres, Meissen, and Wedgewood collected by the Palazzo Pitti's wealthy tenants. The museum's terrace also offers fine prospects across the Tuscan countryside south of Florence.

☻ MUSEO ZOOLOGICO LA SPECOLA

☎ 055 228 82 51; Via Romana 17; admission €4; ☻ 9am-1pm Thu-Tue, until 5pm Sat

This charmingly fusty zoological museum is a taxidermist's dream, with room after room of stuffed

Heading inside to encounter the treasures of the many museums in the Palazzo Pitti

animals of every shape, size and origin. The strong of stomach should not miss its macabre collection of wax sculptures of human bodies dissected and in various states of disease. The hall of horrors was created to train 19th-century medical students.

PALAZZO PITTI ✓

☎ 055 238 86 16; Piazza de' Pitti; €12 (incl Galleria d'Arte Moderna, Galleria Palatina, Appartamenti Reali), €10 (incl Galleria del Costume, Museo degli Argenti, Museo delle Porcellane, Museo delle Carrozze, Giardino Boboli); ☼ 8.15am-6.50pm Tue-Sun (Galleria d'Arte Moderna, Galleria Palatina, Appartamenti Reali), 8.15am-4.30pm Nov-Jan, 8.30am-5.30pm Mar, 8.15am-6.30pm Apr-May & Sep-Oct, 8.15am-7.30pm Jun-Aug (Galleria del Costume, Museo degli Argenti, Museo delle Porcellane, Museo delle Carrozze, Giardino Boboli)

At the insistence of his fussy wife Eleonora de Toledo who was displeased with the Medici quarters in the Palazzo Vecchio, Cosimo I purchased this palazzo in the 1540s from the Pitti, a rival banking family fallen on hard times. The Medici expanded it many times over the centuries, but remarkably, the military bearing of its original, rusticated facade was always respected. Today, the sprawling palazzo contains six separate museums. Three are devoted to the decorative arts, including the Museo degli Argenti (Silver Museum), the Galleria del Costume (Costume Gallery) with displays of fashion and theatrical costumes from the 16th century to present, and the elaborately gilded conveyances of the Museo delle Carrozze (Carriage Museum). The Appartamenti Reali (Royal Apartments), originally the private quarters of the Medici, were redone in the height of dubious 19th-century taste for the king of a newly united Italy. The misleadingly named Galleria d'Arte Moderna (Modern Art Gallery) houses Florentine art from the 18th and 19th centuries, most notably works from the Macchiaioli movement – considered a key forerunner of French Impressionism. The real draw, though, is the **Galleria Palatina**, an enviable collection of 16th- to 18th-century art amassed by the Medici and Lorraine dukes.

CENTURIES OF MODERNISATION

Majestically guarding the Arno's south bank, the Porta San Niccolò is the most impressive reminder of the medieval walls that long circled Florence for 500 years. However, in the 19th century, the walls were considered an ugly and backward nuisance, and when the city was named capital of the newly united Italy in 1864, they had to come down.

In fact, it was the city's first makeover since the Renaissance, led by architect and engineer Giuseppe Poggi. He razed the ancient walls and built modern boulevards in their place. Others opened wider, straighter avenues leading into the historic centre, including Via Cavour and Via de' Calzaiuoli. The most radical remake of the urban fabric, however, was the demolition of a labyrinthine neighbourhood to make way for the bombastic Piazza della Repubblica (p49).

Since the early 20th century, there have been few visible changes to the historic centre as a new zeitgeist came to prize the very medieval 'backwardness' that Poggi tried to 'improve.' There are a handful of 20th-century buildings in central Florence, mostly uninspired, though they were largely built to replace ancient structures destroyed during the German occupation of the city during World War II.

Today talk of modernisation revolves around transport systems that can bring people in and out of a 'timeless' historic core – without relying on cars. The new Tramvia (p71), trams that will connect the centre with growing suburbs, is well under way. In addition, only residents of central Florence have the right to enter by car; travellers who drive in must register their car with their hotel or risk an expensive fine. More anti-car measures include talk of expanding the city's car-free zone as well as creating more dedicated cycling routes. Finally, work on a new high-speed train station is also underway, which will replace Santa Maria Novella station as the city's principle long-distance gateway.

Raphaels and Rubens vie for centre stage, though the collection also includes works by Guido Reni, Guercino, Tintoretto, Titian, Veronese, Velasquez, Rubens and Van Dyck.

PORTA SAN NICCOLÒ
Piazza Giuseppe Poggi
Built in the 1320s, the best preserved of the city's medieval gates still stands sentinel on the banks of the Arno. Behind it, a monumental staircase designed by Giuseppe Poggi (p115) winds its way up towards Chiesa di San Miniato al Monte (p109).

VILLA BARDINI
☎ 055 29 48 83; www.bardinipeyron.it, in Italian; Costa San Giorgio 4; ❂ 8.15am-7.30pm Jun-Aug, 8.15am-6.30pm Apr-May & Sep-Oct, 8.15am-5.30pm Mar, 8.15am-4.30pm Nov-Feb
Recently renovated, the 17th- to 19th-century villa in the Giardino di Bardini (p109) hosts some of Florence's most important art exhibitions, plus a museum dedicated to the extravagant work of 20th-century fashion designer Roberto Capucci.

SHOP
MADOVA *Leather*
☎ 055 239 65 26; Via de' Guicciardini 1r
It may look at first glance like just another shop on this touristy stretch, but Madova makes some of the city's finest handcrafted gloves. Expect leather that is supple and designs that range from classic to louche, most of which are produced in the adjacent workshop.

EAT
ANTICA MESCITA SAN NICCOLÒ *Classic Tuscan*   €€
☎ 055 234 28 36; Via San Niccolò 60r; ❂ lunch & dinner Mon-Sat
At just €10, the fine little Tuscan lunch buffet is the big draw at this snug little trattoria, with its rustic wooden booths and beamed ceilings. The food is carefully prepared and classically Florentine, from the *crostini ai fegatini* (crostini with liver pâté) to *arista di maiale* (roast pork). It's near the northeast edge of the Bardini Gardens.

DA RUGGERO
Classic Tuscan   €€
☎ 055 220 542; Via Senese 89r; ❂ lunch & dinner Thu-Mon, closed mid-Jul to mid-Aug
Run by the gracious Corsi family, the menu at this classic Florentine trattoria combines excellent ingredients with an upmost respect for Tuscan tradition, from the *crostini toscani* (Tuscan-style crostini) to *bistecca alla fiorentina* (p21). Making a reservation is recommended.

🍴 I TAROCCHI *Pizza* €
☎ 055 234 39 12; Via dei Renai 12r;
🕑 lunch Tue-Fri, dinner Tue-Sun

With its atmospheric vaulted brick ceiling and darkly wooden booths, this pizzeria is a perennial favourite that has actually improved with the years, according to locals. The thin-crust pizza is excellent and classically Florentine. Try the *mozzarella di bufala* (prized mozzarella made from buffalo milk) with fresh tomatoes and basil or the *sfumato*, with smoked cheeses and meats, plus tangy leafy greens. Both are divine.

🍴 LA MANGIATOIA;
Classic Tuscan €
Via Romana 8r; 🕑 lunch & dinner Tue-Sun

This humble but honest *rosticceria* (caterer selling prepared dishes to go) serves up delicious grilled meats, fresh-made pizzas, hot and cold pasta dishes and grilled and sautéed vegetables to go. For a few euros more, you can eat in the no-frills dining room out back.

🍷 DRINK
🍷 CAFFÈ LA TORRE *Bar*
☎ 055 680 643; Lungarno Benvenuto Cellini 65r; 🕑 10.30am-3.30am

Loud wallpaper and indirect lighting makes everyone look good at this still-trendy riverside spot famous for its generous *aperitivo* buffet. Free wi-fi, jazz-driven DJ sets and a chef who cooks until 3am round out the evening.

🍷 ENOTECA FUORI PORTA
Wine Bar
☎ 055 234 24 83; www.fuoriporta.it, in Italian; Via Monte alle Croci 10r; meals around €25; 🕑 noon-midnight Apr-Oct, noon-midnight Mon-Sat Jan-Mar, 7am-midnight Mon-Sat Nov-Dec

Set just outside one of the city's medieval gates, this mellow old *enoteca* proffers up to 500 different wines, including dozens by the glass, with a special strength in Tuscan and Piemontese reds. For a light lunch or evening meal, take a seat on the pleasant terrace and order a plate or two from the limited list of pastas, salads and *crostoni* (grilled, open-faced sandwiches).

🍷 JAMES JOYCE *Bar*
☎ 055 658 08 56; Lungarno Benvenuto Cellini 1r; 🕑 6pm-2am, until 3pm Fri & Sat

Neither as Irish nor as literary as the name suggests, this bar-cum-beer garden attracts a gregarious student and post-grad crowd with its large outdoor terrace, Guinness on tap, table football and requisite U2 soundtrack.

▼ LE VOLPI E L'UVA *Bar*

☎ 055 239 81 32; www.levolpieluva.com;
Piazza de' Rossi 1; ⏲ 11am-9pm Mon-Sat
For its excellent selection of lesser-known vintages, Le Volpi e l'Uva is a must for serious oenophiles. A trim, contemporary decor, short menu of panini and *salumi* (cheeses and meats), and terrace seating on a beautiful little square encourage patrons to linger.

▼ NEGRONI *Bar*

☎ 055 243 647; www.negronibar.com;
Via dei Renai 17r; ⏲ 8am-2am Mon-Sat,
6pm-2am Sun
Negroni shakes up cocktails galore, including its namesake invented in the 1920s, so the story goes, when Florentine Count Camillo Negroni asked the barman at Caffè Giacosa (p69) to add gin to his Americano. To make it at home: shake equal parts gin, Campari and red Martini. The clientele tends to be 30-and-up and well-heeled, and at weekends DJs get them dancing by 11pm or so.

▼ PLASMA *Bar*

☎ 055 051 69 26; www.virtualplasma.it;
Piazza F Ferrucci 1r; ⏲ 6.30pm-1.30am
Wed, Thu & Sun, to 2.30am Fri & Sat
Inside this minimalist fiberoptic-lit drinking space, some of the city's best DJs spin cutting-edge electronica. The bourgeois-hip crowd sips cocktails on Level 0 and gets

Enjoying an early evening Florentine tradition at Negroni – the *aperitivi* buffet (p56)

... AND A GLASS OF CHIANTI

A map of Tuscan wine producers reveals a complex patchwork that includes more than 30 DOC denominations, the equivalent of France's AOC labelling to ensure origin, varietals of grapes and quality. Wines designated *vino da tavola* are generally lower quality and don't follow standard practice, and can range from plonk to excellent.

In addition to the DOC denomination, there are six DOCG labels, indicating particularly prized sub-territories that are subject to more stringent controls. Finally, the Chianti DOCG is itself divided into seven sub-categories. Your head is probably spinning, and you haven't even been drinking. Nor have we mentioned the so-called Super Tuscans, which do not adhere to the DOC rules because, for example, they mix Italian and French varietals, though often to stunning effect.

If in doubt, entrust yourself to the experts at *enoteche* (wine bars) such as Le Volpi e l'Uva (opposite) and Enoteca Fuori Porta (p117).

lost in video art projected on eight giant plasma screens on Level 1.

☐ ZOE *Bar*
☎ 055 24 31 11; Via dei Renai 13r;
🕑 3pm-2am Apr-Oct, 6pm-2am Tue-Sun Nov-Mar

With its industrial-chic interior, nickel-clad bar and glowing Venetian-glass lamps, this busy San Niccolò bar fairly heaves with its squadrons of young local punters, who often spill out onto the street in warmer weather. DJs spin electronica most nights.

★ PLAY

 MONTECARLA CLUB
Nightclub
☎ 055 234 02 59; Via de' Bardi 2;
🕑 9.30pm-6am

With its fearsome bouncers, boudoir furnishings, late-night

hours, and multilevel leopard-skin mosh pits, Montecarla exudes Late Empire decadence. Crowds start out almost mainstream but as the evening goes on the gaggles of professional clubbers start to stage their takeover.

WALKING TOUR
A SWATH OF TUSCAN COUNTRYSIDE

Just south of the Arno lies a surprising swath of the Tuscan countryside that reaches almost to the city centre.

This walk begins at the gates of the **Palazzo Pitti (1**, p114). If time allows, take advantage of the fact that the entrance to the gardens also includes three of the Pitti's decorative arts museums. They sit off the palazzo's remarkable mannerist-style **Cortile di Ammanati**

(**2**), by the eponymous sculpture and architect. After entering the Giardino di Boboli, head first to the **Grotto di Buontalenti** (**3**, p113), an artificial cave filled with goddesses and nymphs – and a great work of mannerist art. Return via the elegant Renaissance **amphitheatre** (**4**, p113), with its central original Egyptian obelisk, and then head right towards the majestic **Viale dei Cipressi** (Avenue of the Cypresses, **5**, p112). Make your way all the way down to **Isolotto** (**6**, p112), an ornamental pond adorned with a marble Neptune and nymphs and, in warmer weather, a wealth

of citrus trees. Return uphill, exploring the shady byways along the Viale dei Cipressi. At the high-point of the gardens, the **Museo delle Porcellane** (**7**, p113) displays exquisite Medici porcelains as well as fine prospects from its front terrace.

Next, wind your way around the walls of the **Forte di Belevedere** (**8**, p109) to its main entrance. Inside, its ramparts offer great panoramic views. From here, head downhill to the steeply pitched and highly manicured **Giardino di Bardini** (**9**, p109), which also provide wonderful city views.

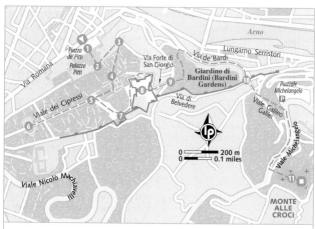

distance: 1.5km **duration**: 2 hours ▶ **start** Palazzo Pitti ● **end** Chiesa di San Miniato al Monte 🚌 13 to/from Santa Maria Novella station

You'd have to be made of stone to turn your back on this view from the Giardino di Bardini (p112)

Exit at the garden's lower reaches and make your way past the Renaissance palazzi that line Via de' Bardi until you reach **Porta San Miniato (10)**, a set of gates in the city's old medieval walls. From here, a cobblestone pedestrian path climbs up to a busy avenue. Turn right and head towards your final stop, **Chiesa di San Miniato al Monte (11**, p109), a sublime Romanesque church with yet more panoramic views across Florence.

>OLTRARNO

Oltrarno literally means 'beyond the Arno', but it's more than a river that sets these quarters apart from the rest of Florence. Both the city's most charming neighbourhood and its most enigmatic, it marries leftist agitation and elegant shopping, dazzling palazzi and humble working-class digs, mum-and-dad trattorias and sleek temples of gastronomy. Artisans, who practise their ancient crafts in dusty storefront workshops, form a kind of natural aristocracy (p19). And a buzzing, student-driven nightlife can be found amid villagelike back streets. Except for the Cappella Brancacci (opposite), the Oltrarno lacks the greatest-hits attractions so common across the river, leaving sidewalks pleasantly unmobbed – except for the congested corridor between the Ponte Vecchio and Palazzo Pitti. Watch sunset from the Ponte Santa Trínita (p17). Then keep heading south and claim a seat on Piazza Santo Spirito, the neighbourhood's ancient heart, to watch as the neighbourhood's social complexities play out over the course of an evening.

OLTRARNO

Please see over for map

◔ SEE

◔ BASILICA DI SANTO SPIRITO

☎ 055 210 030; Piazza Santo Spirito;
⏱ 9.30am-12.30pm, 4-6pm Thu-Tue

Behind a simple plaster facade lies one of Brunelleschi's last and greatest works. Designed in 1434, the church's light-flooded nave is lined by a series of semicircular chapels, while the colonnade of grey Corinthian columns lends a grandeur that is at once harmonious and severe. While a fire in 1471 destroyed much of the art, the church does harbour several masterpieces, including Filipino Lippi's *Madonna con il Bambino e Santi* (Madonna with Child and Saints) in the Cappella Nerli in the right transept. And in the sacristy there's a poignantly tender wooden crucifix attributed to Michelangelo with a rare depiction of Christ's penis. Beneath the central dome, the altar is a voluptuous baroque flourish that is rather out of place in the sparse setting of Brunelleschi's church. Note that opening hours of the church are notoriously erratic.

◔ CAPPELLA BRANCACCI

☎ 055 276 82 24; Piazza del Carmine; €4;
⏱ 10am-5pm Mon & Wed-Sat, 1-5pm Sun

Inside the rather workaday baroque finery of Basilica di Santa Maria del

An evening at the Piazza Santo Spirito is an integral Florence experience

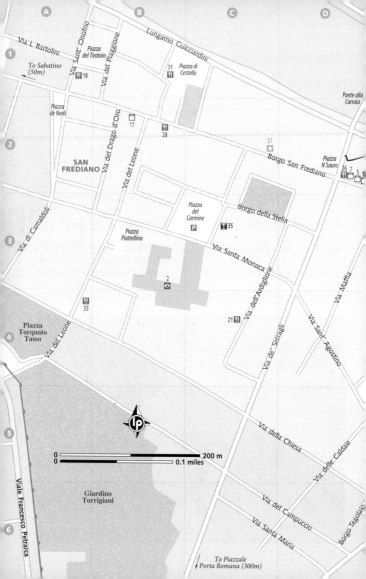

A B C D

Via L Bartolini

Via Sant' Onofrio

Piazza del Tiratoio

Via del Piaggione

Lungarno Guicciardini

Piazza di Cestello

To Sabatino (50m)

18

31

Ponte alla Carraia

Piazza de Nelli

17

28

37

Borgo San Frediano

Piazza N Sauro

26 7

5

SAN FREDIANO

Via del Drago d'Oro

Via del Leone

Borgo della Stella

Piazza del Carmine

P

35

Via di Camaldoli

Piazza Piattellina

2

Via Santa Monaca

Via dell'Ardiglione

Via Santa Agostino

Via Maffia

33

Via de' Serragli

21

Piazza Torquato Tasso

Via del Leone

Via della Chiesa

Via delle Caldaie

200 m

0.1 miles

Giardino Torrigiani

Via del Campuccio

Via Santa Maria

Borgo Tegolaio

Viale Francesco Petrarca

To Piazzale Porta Romana (300m)

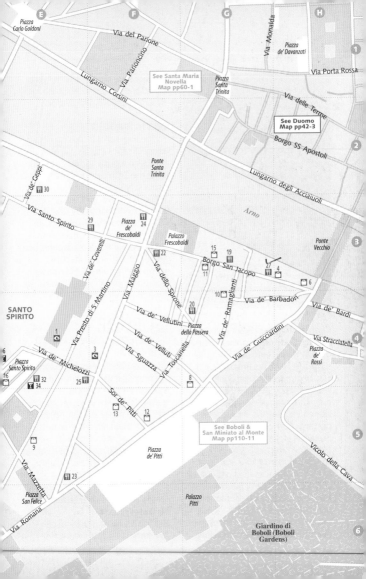

SEEING RED

Long a stronghold of the Italian left, Florence can trace its socialist roots all the way to the Middle Ages. In 1378 labourers in the city's wool industry, many of whom lived in the working-class quarters of the Oltrarno, staged a successful if short-lived revolution that gave them political representation in a city that had long been dominated by rich merchants. With the rapid industrialisation of the early 20th century, the leftward slant returned in the form of a strong trade union movement. Tuscany also proved an important centre for the growing resistance to Mussolini's rule in the 1930s. Still today, the city regularly votes for leftist candidates in both local and national elections.

Carmine, the small Brancacci chapel harbours one of the great treasures of early Renaissance art. Commissioned in 1424, the fresco cycle was begun by Masolino, but it's the work of his pupil Masaccio, then only 22, that makes art historians launch into paeans. His most important contributions include *The Expulsion of Adam and Eve*, *Tribute Money*, *St Peter Healing the Sick* and *The Distribution of Alms and Death of Ananias*. Besides their naturalism and successful use of perspective, Masaccio's depiction of emotion – particularly Eve's anguish – lends the cycle a remarkable combination of immediacy and humanity. Res-

ervations are required as visits are timed and limited to small groups. Reserve ahead in high season.

◎ VIA MAGGIO

As the line-up of imposing Renaissance facades attests, Via Maggio has been a posh address since at least the 16th century. The street is especially beautiful at night, when you can look up and see glimpses of frescoed ceilings. By day, Via Maggio does a brisk business in high-end antiques. Check out Traslucido at No 9r for Japanese and art deco finery, Massimo Vezzosi at No 60r for old master paintings, and Il Cartiglio at No 78r for Renaissance-era furnishings.

SHOP

◎ A PIEDI NUDI NEL PARCO
Clothing

☎ 055 265 82 21; Borgo San Jacopo 38r; ⏱ 10am-8pm Mon-Sat, 11am-7pm Sun

Specialising in high-end avant-garde designers, this riverside shop may cause sticker shock with its industrial-chic duds for both men and women. However, you're certain to take away something no one else at the office is wearing.

◎ ANGELA CAPUTI *Jewellery*

☎ 055 212 972; www.angelacaputi.com; Via Santo Spirito 58r

Behind a wall of glass you can see Angela Caputi's workshop,

Angela Caputi
Jeweller, designer, impresario

For nearly a millennium, Florence has made its living from beautiful things. According to jeweller Angela Caputi (shop details opposite), artisans here still possess a unique drive to 'unite a mode of thinking with the way they work with their hands'. Unlike many colleagues who inherited their trade, Caputi is a first-generation artisan. Another departure from tradition: her boldly vivid jewellery is made from plastics in a city that tends to favour natural materials. 'For me it is a kind of game to give natural shapes to an industrial product – to make it something 'more' than it is,' she says. Caputi gets offers to open stores in Paris and New York, but always refuses. She prefers to stay small in order to maintain direct physical contact, both with her customers and her work. 'This contact, this sense of touch, is central to the Florentine tradition,' she says. And a fellow artisan Caputi particularly admires? Stefano Bemer (p130).

where she and her team fashion her distinctive, contemporary jewellery. Her favourite material is plastic, which she transforms into unlikely shapes, often inspired by natural materials and forms. Despite her worldwide reputation, the prices of smaller pieces are surprisingly within reach of a modest budget.

BEATRICE GALLI *Accessories*
☎ 055 289 193; Borgo San Jacopo 24r
In her neatly diminutive shop just a few yards from the Ponte Vecchio, Signora Galli offers up locally produced yarns in a complex rainbow of colours and materials.

FRANCESCO DA FIRENZE
Shoes
☎ 055 212 428; Via Santo Spirito 62r;
🕒 closed two weeks Aug
Jolly Francesco and his crew hammer out fine men's footwear in the dusty workshop just behind their slightly less dusty shop. He provides ready-to-wear models as well as made-to-measure kicks at surprisingly nonastronomical rates.

GIULIO GIANNINI & FIGLIO
Stationery
☎ 055 212 621; Piazza de' Pitti 37r;
🕒 10am-7pm, closed Sun Jan & Feb
Among the city's premiere stationers, this snugly old-fashioned, family-run outfit produces hand-

Shops in Florence combine style and flair in their design as well as their wares, as seen at Quelle Tre

marbled paper, clever engravings, leather-bound notebooks and made-to-order products such as invitations and calling cards.

☐ MILLESIMI *Food & Wine*
☎ 055 265 46 75; Borgo Tegolaio 33r; ☽ noon-8pm Mon-Fri, 10.30am-8pm Sat & 2nd Sun of month

Ring the bell and wait for staff to open Millesimi's vast, wood-carved door, behind which lies perhaps the finest collection of wines in the city. The Franco-Italian couple that run the shop stock their cellars not just with the best Italian and French vintages but also a distinctly unsnobbish selection of excellent labels for under €20 a bottle.

☐ MM *Leather*
☎ 055 283 870; www.monacometro politano.com; Via de' Ramaglianti 6r

Leathergoods in Florence may be of high quality, but designs can grow repetitive. Not so at MM (also known as Monaco Metropolitano), which offers bags, belts and brace-lets in creatively natural shapes and textures. You can often watch craftsmen cutting, tooling and sewing the exquisite leathers right inside the shop's door.

☐ OBSEQUIUM *Food & Wine*
☎ 055 216 849; www.obsequium.it; Borgo San Jacopo 39r

Occupying the ground floor of one the city's best-preserved medieval towers, this shop offers a wide range of fine Tuscan wines and foodstuffs displayed becomingly across several gleaming rooms. Depending on the availability of staff, a tasting room in back offers a chance to sample wines, olive oils and other Tuscan treats.

☐ PITTI MOSAICI *Furnishings*
☎ 055 282 127; Piazza dei Pitti 23r; ☽ 10am-7pm Mon-Sat, 11am-6pm Sun

Gawk at the fine art of *pietre dure* – exquisite mosaics made from mar-ble and semiprecious stones – inside this shop just across from the Palazzo Pitti. Wares range from geometric tabletops to trompe l'oeil still lives.

☐ PITTI VINTAGE *Clothing*
☎ 055 230 26 76; Sor de' Pitti; ☽ 4-7.30pm Mon, 10am-1.30pm, 3.30-7.30pm Tue-Sat, 3-7.30pm 2nd & 3rd Sun of month

Specialising in couture from the 1970s and '80s, this shop offers one of the largest collections of vintage duds this side of the Arno. Expect quality rather than second-hand bargains.

☐ QUELLE TRE *Accessories*
☎ 055 219 374; Via Santo Spirito 42r; ☽ 10.30am-2pm, 3-7pm Tue-Sat

Three sisters join forces to create their own line of quirkily elegant

NEIGHBOURHOODS

OLTRARNO

Shoes on show at Stefano Bemer

clothing and accessories that combine fine natural fabrics, Bohemian cuts and vivid colours and prints.

🏠 SAN JACOPO SHOW
Furnishings
☎ 239 69 12; Borgo San Jacopo 66r
This category-busting shop began as a showroom for handmade mannequins but has expanded to include fashion-forward fabrics, decoupage furnishings and original art and photography.

🏠 SANTO SPIRITO ORGANIC MARKET *Market*
Piazza Santo Spirito; ☼ 3rd Sun of month
This monthly market attracts artisans and organic farmers from around Tuscany, with stands devoted to fresh produce, hand-painted crockery, spices gathered from Chianti hillsides and much more.

🏠 STEFANO BEMER *Shoes*
☎ 055 222 558; www.bemers.it; Borgo San Frediano 143r
Men's footwear doesn't get better than this. The shop's brochure justifies the extravagance this way: 'Quality is remembered long after price is forgotten.' Combining classic designs with a modern flair, Bemer produces both made-to-measure and prêt-á-porter models. Materials range from English suede to the skins of crocodiles, ostriches, stingrays and, yes, toads.

🍴 EAT

🍴 ALL'ANTICO RISTORO DI' CAMBI *Classic Tuscan*   €€
☎ 055 217 134; Via Sant'Onofrio 1r;
☼ lunch & dinner Mon-Sat, closed Aug
Founded as a wine shop in 1950, this Oltrarno institution sticks closely to the traditional, with its long list of fine Tuscan wines, dried meats hanging from brick-vaulted ceilings, and a glass case proudly displaying its highly regarded *bistecca alla fiorentina* (p21).

🍴 BORGO SAN JACOPO

Italian €€€€

☎ 055 281 661; Borgo San Jacopo 62r;
🕐 dinner Wed-Mon, closed Aug

Part of the Salvatore Ferragamo empire, this swish riverside restaurant marries a stylish cream-and-white interior with fashionable Arno views. Chef Beatrice Segoni (p132) whips up a wonderful combination of contemporary and traditional dishes, with a special penchant for seafood. Try the citrus-marinated mackerel, pasta stuffed with scallops, celeriac and chicory, or fritters with feta mousse. Reservations recommended.

🍴 CAFFÈ DEGLI ARTIGIANI

Italian €

☎ 055 291 882; Via dello Sprone 16r;
🕐 7am-7pm Mon, 7am-1am Tue-Sat, closed Aug

Sitting on one of the most atmospheric little piazzas in Florence, this quaintly countrified cafe pulls in local artisans in need of an espresso hit or nip of brandy to complete a day's work. In the small dining room, which seems to have been plucked from a Provençal farmhouse, you can enjoy quick eats such as sandwiches and homemade cakes. Even more inviting is the handful of outdoor tables.

All'Antico Ristoro di' Cambi offers classic Tuscan meals in classic Tuscan surrounds

Beatrice Segoni
Executive chef, Borgo San Jacopo

Men have long ruled high-end Florentine kitchens, but a new generation of women chefs is stirring the pot. 'There's still rivalry with male colleagues,' admits Beatrice Segoni, who runs the highly regarded Borgo San Jacopo (p131). 'They can treat you with froideur. But that's just because they're a little afraid.' **What intimidates them?** 'As wives and mothers, we learn to do many things at once, whereas they can only handle one task at a time.' For Segoni, originally from the Marche region, Tuscan food has a special genius. 'First, there is its simplicity. The ingredients are so good that all we have to do is exalt them. Then there is the care Tuscans take with meat, such as *bistecca alla fiorentina* and *cinta senesa* (a special breed of Sienese pork). Finally I have to mention their wonderful soups.' **Another female chef to watch out for?** Segoni singles out Giovanna Iorio of Alle Murate (p100).

🍴 CAVOLO NERO
Contemporary Tuscan   €€€

☎ 055 294 744; Via dell' Ardiglione 22;
🕑 dinner Mon-Sat, closed Aug

Tucked up a tiny residential backstreet, this favourite of local foodies has evolved beyond its classic Florentine roots and now includes contemporary takes on dishes from around Italy. Try the risotto with radicchio and red wine or linguini with calamari, white beans and sage. Behind the clubby little dining room lies an outdoor terrace under a canopy of jasmine vines. Reservations recommended.

🍴 DA CAMILLO *Italian*   €€€

☎ 055 212 963; Borgo San Jacopo 57r;
🕑 lunch & dinner Thu-Mon

Buzzing with good cheer, this wonderful trattoria is spread over a honeycomb of cosy dining rooms. The kitchen, run with aplomb by Chiara Masiero, is less traditional than the bow-tied staff would suggest. It has a long menu that includes a number of seafood dishes as well as classic pastas, roast meats and house specialities such as *ceciata di maile* (fragrant pork stew). Reservations highly recommended.

🍴 DOLCISSIMO *Bakery*

☎ 055 239 62 68; Via Maggio 61r;
🕑 8am-8pm Tue-Sat, 9am-2pm Sun

Except for the self-service espresso machine and yellow lizard-skin banquette, this little *pasticceria* (pastry shop) is unapologetically old-fashioned, with its glass chandelier, gold-trimmed display cases and rich, French-influenced fruit tarts, *mignons* (mini-pastries) and extravagant cakes.

🍴 GELATERIA SANTA TRÍNITA
Gelato

Lungarno Guicciardini; 🕑 11.30am-11pm

The newest addition to Florence's list of excellent gelato makers, this shop just off the Ponte Santa Trínita produces a small selection of gelati that manages to achieve the perfect balance of sweetness and creaminess.

🍴 GUSTAPIZZA *Pizza*   €

☎ 055 285 068; Via Maggio 46r;
🕑 dinner Mon-Sat, closed Aug

Order your pizza at the counter and then take a seat at one of the glass-topped wine casks that serve as tables at this brand new spot a block off Piazza Santo Spirito. Service is brusque but the pizza, with its medium-to-thick crust and baked in a traditional wood oven, is unimpeachably good.

🍴 IL RISTORO
Classic Tuscan   €€

☎ 055 264 55 69; Borgo San Jacopo 48r;
🕑 11am-9pm

Angle for the riverside seats at this bright, casually minimalist and surprisingly economical self-service eatery, which sits just a skip and a jump from the Ponte Vecchio. The menu includes salads, classic Tuscan soups and pastas, most of which cost well under €10.

🍴 IL SANTO BEVITORE 26
Contemporary Tuscan   €€€
☎ 055 211 264; Via Santo Spirito 64r;
🕐 lunch & dinner, closed Aug
Favoured by youthful foodies who've saved up their pennies for something more enticing than pizza, Il Santo Bevitore offers good value for money, includ-

ing carefully crafted cheese and *salumi* (cured meat), savoury pastas and steak tartare using prized Chianina beef. The menu is complemented by a list of well-priced wines.

🍴 MIGNANI RODOLFO
Self-catering
Borgo San Frediano 127r; 🕐 **7am-1pm, 5-7.30pm Mon-Sat**
Practically a museum of meat, this old-fashioned *macelleria* (butcher) offers up top-quality meat amid spotlessly polished marble interior. Your source for much-valued Chianina beef.

The inviting dining room of Olio & Convivium restaurant

🍴 OLIO & CONVIVIUM

Contemporary Tuscan   €€

☎ 055 265 81 98; Via Santo Spirito 4;
🕐 10am-3pm Mon, 10am-3pm & 5.30-
10.30pm Tue-Sat

Offering treats such as wild boar prosciuttos and truffle conserves, this trim little gastronomic shop also has a sparking little dining room where you can enjoy a €15 lunchtime menu that includes a cold mixed platter, wine, water and dessert. Or you can spring for the á la carte menu, which offers dishes such as veal-stuffed fresh artichokes or taglierini with tiger prawns and black cabbage.

🍴 RISTORANTE BECCOFINO

Contemporary Tuscan   €€€

☎ 055 290 076; Piazza degli Scarlatti 1r;
🕐 dinner Tue-Sun

After a tour of duty with French master Alain Ducasse, chef Roberto Pepin is back in the saddle at this contemporary eatery that sits on a pleasant little piazza just off the Arno. In addition to an unusual amount of elbowroom in the sleek, airy dining space, Pepin serves clever updates of Tuscan classics. Try the perfectly prepared *tagliata* (sliced tenderloin of beef) or the cleverly inventive shrimp salad with potatoes, fava beans and *agretti* (tart, grasslike greens). Making a reservation is recommended.

🍴 RISTORANTE PANE E VINO

Contemporary Tuscan   €€€

☎ 055 247 69 56; Piazza di Cestello 3r;
🕐 dinner Mon-Sat, closed 2 weeks Aug

A live video feed from the kitchen is projected on TV screens around the restaurant, and when you taste the food you'll forgive the gimmick. At €45, the four-course tasting menu is practically a bargain. Swoon over sardines in liquorice sauce, *baccalà in brandade* (salt cod pâté) and *quaglie fritte* (fried quail). Finish with the simple but unforgettable *panna cotta* (baked cream) with almonds and caramel. Service is not always at the same quality of the food. Reservations recommended.

🍴 RISTORANTE RICCHI

Seafood   €€€

☎ 055 215 864; Piazza Santo Spirito 8r;
🕐 dinner Mon-Sat

Perched on Piazza Santo Spirito, this Oltrarno institution specialises in contemporary seafood dishes such as tuna tartare with strawberries and balsamic vinegar gelatine, or zucchini flowers stuffed with ricotta and calamari and served over a creamy concoction of grilled red peppers. The experience is especially delightful when consumed on a warm evening on the restaurant's terrace, which sits right on the piazza. Unfortunately service can be overly casual.

🍴 SABATINO *Classic Tuscan* €
☎ 055 225 955; Via Pisana 2r; ⌚ lunch & dinner Mon-Fri, closed Aug
Once a barely salubrious hole in the wall, this family-run trattoria has gotten a makeover to meet EU regulations. Fortunately, its prices remain stuck in time, as does its menu of heartily humble Tuscan home cooking such as dead-simple pasta dishes and oven-roasted meats.

🍴 VEGETUS *Vegetarian* €
☎ 055 214 722; Via del Leone 53r; ⌚ 10am-10pm; 🅥
Vegetarians and their friends should seek out this colourfully cheery little eatery for its organic, meat-free menu that includes savoury soups, salads and cheese torts.

🍸 DRINK
🍸 CAFFÈ RICCHI *Cafe*
☎ 055 215 864; Piazza Santo Spirito 8r; ⌚ 7am-10pm Mon-Sat, 8am-10pm Sun, closed Sun Oct-Apr
Smack on Piazza Santo Spirito, this Bohemian cafe has lined its walls with works by local artists, including a series of clever takes on the blank facade of Brunelleschi's adjacent church. In warm weather, the terrace seating can't be beat, and the gelato is the best in the neighbourhood.

🍸 LA DOLCE VITA *Bar*
☎ 055 284 595; Piazza del Carmine 6r; ⌚ 5pm-2am Tue-Sun, closed 2 weeks Aug
Perennial favourite of the city's status-conscious youth and nearly young, Dolce Vita has stood up to competition from newer offerings such as Noir (p69) and Colle Beretto (p55) and remains the best place to show off your prowess in selecting designer labels. As weather permits, crowds spill out of the industrial-style interior onto

FLORENCE BOHEMIA
Despite rising rents, the Oltrarno district remains the headquarters of the city's alternative scene. Restaurants and cafes tend to double as art galleries, while tattoos, piercings and Euro-dreads are on proud display. Each evening, the young and youthful in various states of revolt gather in the piazza in front of **Basilica di Santo Spirito** (p123), where a few friends and a bottle of wine make an evening. **Pop Café** (opposite) is a central meeting point for those that can afford cocktails, while bookstore-cafe **Libreria Café La Cité** (opposite) puts on free cultural events ranging from tango lessons to experimental theatre. Artists, artisans and their admirers gather at **Caffè degli Artigiani** (p131). And cheap eats at places such as **La Mangiatoia** (p117) and **Sabatino** (left) keep starving students well fed.

the adjacent piazza, which would be stunning if it weren't made to double as a car park.

▼ POP CAFÉ *Bar*
☎ 055 213 852; Piazza Santo Spirito 18r;
☽ noon-2am

A major draw for Oltrarno hipsters, this bar features art-lined walls, a daily vegetarian *aperitivo* buffet, and Sunday brunch from 12.30pm to 3pm. After 10pm most nights its boisterous crowds merge seamlessly with the drunks and punks who have made the Piazza Santo Spirito their preferred after-dark venue.

 ## PLAY
☆ LIBRERIA CAFÉ LA CITÉ
Nightclub
☎ 055 210 387; www.lacitelibreria
.info, in Italian; Borgo San Frediano 20r;
☽ 11.30am-midnight Tue-Sat, 3.30pm-midnight Sun & Mon

Already an institution of Oltrarno cultural life, this combination cafe, bookstore and cultural centre was founded by a collective of young Florentine intellectuals. Sip an espresso, access the free wi-fi, read in the quiet mezzanine, or attend the free evening events that usually include jazz jam sessions on Monday, tango lessons on Tuesday, literary readings on Wednesday, theatre and dance on Thursday, and live music Friday and Saturday.

WALKING TOUR
HANDMADE FLORENCE

Most travellers come to Florence in search of antique splendours. But even in our factory-made 21st century, the backstreets of the Oltrarno harbour a living tradition of men and women creating beautiful objects by hand.

This walk starts out at one of the city's very finest workshops, **Stefano Bemer** (**1**, p130), which produces exquisite men's shoes by hand. At nearby **Mignani Rodolfo** (**2**, p134), meat is chosen, prepared and displayed with an artist's eye. Down the street, **Francesco di Firenze** (**3**, p128) also produces made-to order men's shoes at surprisingly accessible prices. Next door, **Angela Caputi** (**4**, p126) wows with her plastic-based jewellery, all made on the premises. A few doors away, three sisters sell their handcrafted, colourfully contemporary women's clothes and accessories at **Quelle Tre** (**5**, p129).

Heading east, you pass Via Maggio and suddenly the street grows thick with high-end storefronts. The difficult-to-categorise **San Jacopo Show** (**6**, p130) is a must-stop, with its collection of exquisite fabrics and hand-fashioned mannequins. A quick detour up a beautiful backstreet lands you at **MM** (**7**, p129), which combines a store and leather workshop in one

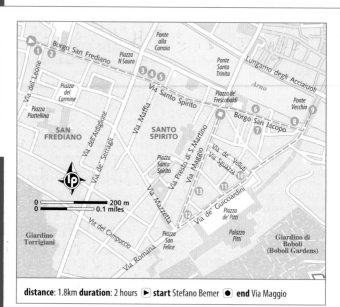

distance: 1.8km **duration**: 2 hours ▶ **start** Stefano Bemer ● **end** Via Maggio

beautiful space. Back on Borgo San Jacopo, **Beatrice Galli** (**8**, p128) offers do-it-yourself types gorgeous, locally made yarns.

As you reach the **Ponte Vecchio** (**9**, p50), the stakes grow higher amid its tiny shops resplendent with hand-crafted gold jewellery. Next, follow the crowds down Via de' Guicciardini, where you'll find Florence's best stationer, **Giulio**

Giannini & Figlio (**10**, p128), followed quickly by the mind-bogglingly complex *pietre dure* (p89) mosaics of **Pitti Mosaici** (**11**, p129).

It's time for a pitstop at **Dolcissimo** (**12**, p133), with its carefully crafted baked goods. Once you've refuelled, explore the exquisite work of artisans past in the high-end antique stores that line **Via Maggio** (**13**, p126).

Another tourist confirms that the tower in Pisa (p142) does indeed lean

FIESOLE #7 bus orange

Before there was Florence, there was Fiesole. Today its unrivalled vistas are shared between local elites in their hillside palazzi and day-trippers from Florence. But for centuries, it was the exclusive domain of Etruscans, who held sway for more than four centuries until the upstart Romans swiped their land in the 3rd century BC. Remains of both civilizations are still very much in evidence here.

So are the panoramic views that have made Fiesole a strategic prize for ancient warriors and contemporary amblers alike. Try to time your visit to coincide with sunset, when the westerly sun burnishes Florence and the surrounding hills with picture-book golds and pinks.

From Piazza Mino da Fiesole, the town's main square, staggering views are just a short, steep walk up Via San Francesco. From here, Florence is laid out before you, capped of course by Brunelleschi's serene dome (p12). A series of tree-lined terraces invite picnicking or just plain ogling. Up the same hill hide a pair of remarkable churches. The plain exterior of **Sant'Alessandro** hides contemporary art exhibitions as well as sensuous *marmorino cipollino* (onion marble) columns inside. The Gothic **San Francesco** has been over-restored but remains a lovely retreat from the afternoon sun, as do the adjacent **Giardini Pubblici** (Public Gardens), with shady walks though no views to speak of.

Back down on the main piazza, the town's Romanesque **cathedral** was practically the only building spared when Florentines took over the city in 1125. Inside, supporting columns incorporate capitals filched from Roman temples. For a more comprehensive insight into Roman Fiesole, you'll find **Area Archeologica** just around the corner. Its most impressive site is its ancient amphitheatre, which still hosts summer shows and concerts during the **Estate Fiesolana** (p28) festival. The stage's backdrop – stunning views across a steep valley of farms and olive orchards towards the foothills of the Apennines – is worth the price of admission. Wander around the remains of Roman baths and the little museum with exhibits from the Bronze Age to Roman periods.

Admission into the Area Archeologica also includes the adjacent **Museo Bandini**, a sweet little museum with a collection of 13th- to 15th-century Tuscan art, including a renowned *Annunciazione* (Annunciation) by Taddeo Gaddi. For art of a different sort, seek out the relatively modest Renaissance **Villa le Coste**, once home of prominent Italian Futurist Primo

Conti and now the principle showcase of his work.

Select villas that blanket Fiesole's hillsides occasionally open their gates. Visiting hours are haphazard, so check at the town tourist office, located next to the Area Archeologica. The Renaissance-style gardens of **Villa Peyron** are particularly impressive.

The tourist office has good, free maps of walks in the surrounding countryside. Fiesole is also the jumping-off point for more ambitious hikes that make up what is called the **Anello del Rinascimento** (Renaissance Ring). It includes 170km of trails that circle the hills, valleys and villages that ring greater Florence. The Comune di Firenze tourist office (p181) provides a decent topographical map.

There is a decent if uninspired range of restaurants and eateries on Piazza Mino da Fiesole.

INFORMATION
Location 8km north of Florence
Getting there ATAF (Florence municipal) bus 7 (€1.20, 30 minutes, every 20 minutes) runs from Stazione di Santa Maria Novella in Florence to Piazza Mino da Fiesole in Fiesole.
Contact www.comune.fiesole.fi.it, in Italian; ☎ 055 59 87 20; Via Portigiani 3

PISA

These days Pisa is a quaint university town that would have been forgotten by history except for one famously odd tower. Yet during the 11th and 12th centuries, the city grew quickly into a powerful maritime republic that was a rival of Venice and Genoa in the struggle to control the Mediterranean. The city's extraordinary cathedral square, dubbed Campo dei Miracoli (Field of Miracles), pays lavish testament to these glories days.

Of course the Campo's most famous feature is its **Torre Pendente** (Leaning Tower). Begun in 1173, it had already started to list within a few years, thanks to an undersized foundation and shifting subsoil. Despite such inauspicious beginnings, the city spent the next several hundred years trying to make good on their original investment. New floors added in the 1270s were purposely built unevenly, so that the leaning tower actually curves subtly back to centre.

Ultimately, Pisan persistence paid off. Today, the sight attracts millions of visitors, most bussed in for a quick snapshot and purchase of a replica key chain, then bussed back out again. Recent, successful efforts at reinforcing the precarious tower has enabled visitors to climb the tower once again, though the limited numbers make reservations a must (www .opapisa.it/boxoffice).

Needless to say, bus tours miss a great deal during their 20-minute stops. The adjacent buildings on the Campo dei Miracoli represent a unique mix of Romanesque, Byzantine and Arab elements – a perfect reflection of Pisa's far-flung maritime interests. Yet master sculptors and architects married these elements into a harmonious whole that is thoroughly Pisan. Reinforcing this stylistic coherence was the fact that the complex was largely built within a single century.

Just behind the leaning tower, Pisa's **duomo** (cathedral) was begun in 1064 and paid for with booty from a raid on an Arab fleet in Sicily. The facade is pure Pisan-Gothic, with four exquisite tiers of columns diminishing upwards. Its doors depict palm trees, Moorish buildings and other Arab motifs. Inside, Giovanni Pisano's octagonal pulpit is a masterpiece that helped usher in a new pictorial language for Gothic sculpture.

Two other peculiar structures complete this unusual complex. The **Camposanto**, a walled cemetery containing soil snatched from Calvary during the Crusades, serves as the resting place for prominent medieval Pisans, many buried in recycled Roman sarcophagi. And the perfectly round **Battistero** (Baptistery) possesses an Arab-style floor and a proto-Renaissance pulpit inspired by sarcophagi from the adjacent cemetery.

Regrettably, a large portion of Pisa's historic centre was destroyed during World War II. Still, it's peaceful, curving riverfront is still lovely to behold, while **Piazza delle Vettovaglie** has lively outdoor cafes that attract a goodly number of the 50,000 students from the nearby University of Pisa. As time allows, there are some impressive buildings to explore, all within a short walk. Perched next to the Arno, the postage-stamp-sized **Santa Maria della Spina** church is an ornate little Pisan-Gothic jewel. The theatrical little **Piazza dei Cavalieri**, designed by Florentine architect Giorgio Vasari, served as the city's temporal headquarters. And for a bird's-eye view of the lovely whole, climb the 200 steps of the 14th-century **Torre Guelfa**.

INFORMATION

Location 92km west of Florence
Getting there Trains (www.trenitalia.it) from Santa Maria Novella in Florence serve central Pisa (€5.60, 1¼ hours, 40 daily)
Contact www.comune.pisa.it

IL CHIANTI

With its rolling green hills, olive groves, stone farmhouses and prized grapes, Il Chianti is the stuff that books, movies and dreams are made of. Stretching from just south of Florence all the way to Siena, the region has long been renowned for its namesake Chianti Classico. These days, it's the place where Brits and Americans come to buy decrepit farmhouses, fix them up, write books about their adventures, and then pay off the mortgage by selling the rights to the movie. It could happen to you as well.

Can't stay here that long? Then rent a car or bicycle and go and explore the region for a day or two. The winding SS222 highway takes you through the heart of Chianti country. Note that many vineyards require reservations to visit, so plan ahead if you've got your heart set on one particular tipple.

Heading south from Florence, make Greve in Chianti your first stop. Ground Zero for the Slow Food movement, it's also home to **Le Cantine di Greve in Chianti**, a one-stop shop for tasting more than 100 local wines. From Greve there's also a delightful 3km walk up to **Castello di Montefioralle**, a medieval hilltop village and the birthplace of New World explorer Amerigo Vespucci.

Badia de Passignano, a massive abbey dating to the 11th century, is a worthy detour as you continue to head south. Panzano is home to Dario Cecchini, a legendary butcher and Slow Food favourite who recites Dante as he wields his knife. Nearer Siena, the countryside around Gaiole harbours two famous vineyards, **Castello di Meleto** and **Castello di Brolio**, with its magnificent 11th-century buildings.

INFORMATION

Location 20km (Greve) to 60km (Gaiole) south of Florence
Getting there Get a map of the region from the Florence tourist office (p181), rent a car or bike in Florence and head south along SS222.
Contact Get information about the region from the Provincia di Firenze tourist office (www.firenzeturismo.it).

The enticing colours of autumn, Il Chianti

SIENA

The ancient rivalry between Siena and Florence seems to have been inherited by contemporary travellers, who tend to prefer strongly one at the expense of the other. Siena definitely gets our nod for the quaintest, with its narrow Gothic lanes, roseate stone buildings, easy access to the Tuscan countryside, and above all its car-free historic centre. The city does lack the grand gestures of Renaissance Florence, because by the 15th century Siena had lost ground to its more dynamic rival. Florence eventually took the city in 1557. The good news is that Siena's humbler status helped preserve a medieval urban fabric that hybrid Florence lacks.

Life in Siena is centred on the fan-shaped **Piazza del Campo**. It's arguably Italy's finest main square with its herringbone paving and Gothic marvels such as the Palazzo Pubblico – still the town hall. The piazza also doubles as a racetrack during the legendary Palio races (p30). Held on 2 July and again on 15 August, the races represent the height of Italian pageantry, beginning with a parade of drummers and flag-bearers in period dress and culminating in a no-holds-barred horse race that pits the city's *contrade* (ancient neighbourhoods) against one another.

With the fertile Tuscan countryside beginning almost at the city's edge, food is the other municipal obsession, with **Il Canto de l'Hotel Certosa**

de Maggiano (☎ 0577 28 81 80; www.ilcanto.it; Strada di Certosa 82-86) widely recognised as the city's top restaurant. Don't miss the city's baked goods, especially *ricciarelli* (almond biscuits) and *panforte* (a dense, spicy concoction of candied fruit and nuts).

Even if it lacks the greatest hits of Florence, Siena is rich in its own unique brand of art and architecture. The trove of late-medieval paintings in the **Pinacoteca Nazionale** are a reminder of the city's economic and cultural heyday in the 13th to 14th centuries, when it rivalled Florence as both a banking and textile powerhouse. The paintings of this period combine a nascent realism with beguilingly rich colours and generous use of gold leaf. Keep an eye out for works by Duccio de Buoninsegna and Ambrogio Lorenzetti. Increasingly, art historians consider this so-called Sienese School as a key bridge between medieval and Renaissance painting.

The **cathedral** is another stunning example of the city's salad days. Begun in 1196, it combines Romanesque austerity with Gothic profusion. You can still trace the outlines of a massive expansion that had to be scrapped because of the Black Death in 1348. Inside, the intricately carved, polychrome floors are impressive, though many are covered by wood planks to protect them from wear and tear. Also keep your eyes peeled for Nicola Pisano's 13th-century pulpit and a bronze *John the Baptist* by Donatello in a chapel off the north transept.

The **Palazzo Pubblico**, begun in the 1290s, is a masterpiece of Italian Gothic, with its convex facade mirroring the Piazza del Campo on which it sits. Its Torre del Mangia, which rises 102m, provides staggering views over the city and surrounding countryside for those game to climb 400-plus steps. Or settle for the palazzo's **Museo Civico**, with several rooms decked out in late-medieval frescoes of the distinctive style of the Sienese school. The greatest work is the *Maestá* by Simone Martini, with the Virgin and Child surrounded by a profusion of saints against a rich blue background.

INFORMATION

Location 70km south of Florence
Getting there SITA (www.sitabus.it, in Italian) express buses run from just west of Stazione di Santa Maria Novella in Florence to central Siena (€6.50, 1¼ hours, at least hourly). Local trains are less useful and the Siena station is a distance from the centre.
Contact www.comune.siena.it/ilturista/?lan=ENG; ☎ 0577 28 05 51; Piazza del Campo 56

SAN GIMIGNANO

Approaching San Gimignano through undulating fields, the town's tight concentration of towers periodically looms up like a Middle Ages version of Manhattan. Once numbering as many as 72, the towers were built by medieval grandees. Today only 14 towers are left, but they still create a remarkable sense of drama in a town that, since the 14th century, has been little more than an agrarian outpost of the Florentine empire.

The most beautiful of the Tuscan hill towns, San Gimignano draws crowds that, during summer, weekends and holidays, make it feel like a Tuscan theme park. If you come at these times, try at least to arrive in the early morning, or stay until after the crowds thin in the late afternoon.

The views from its ancient walls look across a fine quilt of fields and orchards. The Romanesque **basilica** is worth the admission, with two remarkable cycles of 14th-century frescoes. Bartolo di Fredi's depicts the main stories of the Old Testament, while Simone Martini's covers the New Testament. Both have a compellingly quirky freshness that belies their age.

INFORMATION

Location 55km southwest of Florence
Getting there SITA (www.sitabus.it, in Italian) buses run from just west of Stazione di Santa Maria Novella in Florence to San Gimignano often involving a quick change in Poggibonsi (€6.20, 1¼ hours, hourly)
Contact www.comune.sangimignano.si.it

LUCCA

Tucked away amid rich farmland near the foot of the Apuane Alps, lovely Lucca has long remained aloof from the rest of Tuscany. The city is girded by an unbroken series of Renaissance walls and bastions. Find a grassy stretch and behold the view across the city's rooftops to mountain peaks.

Founded by Etruscans, Lucca grew in importance during Roman rule. You can still make out the outlines of the Roman amphitheatre in the elliptical **Piazza dell'Anfiteatro**. In the 11th century, the city prospered from silk production, when it built itself its **cathedral**. The facade recalls that of Pisa's, while inside you'll find the pulpit and *tempietto* (little temple) by Matteo Civitali. Other churches worth seeking out include the exuberantly Romanesque **San Michele in Foro**, the over-the-top baroque **Santa Maria Corte-orlandini**, and **San Giovanni e Reparata**, where recently uncovered foundations were found to encompass Roman and early Christian ruins.

Lined with antique palazzi and smart boutiques, **Via Fillungo** is the city's busiest pedestrian thoroughfare.

INFORMATION
Location 72km northwest of Florence
Getting there Trains (www.trenitalia.it) from Santa Maria Novella in Florence serve central Lucca (€5.00, 1½ hours, at least 30 daily)
Contact www.comune.lucca.it, in Italian; ☎ 0583 495 730; Viale Giusti, 100m from the train station

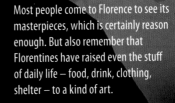

Most people come to Florence to see its masterpieces, which is certainly reason enough. But also remember that Florentines have raised even the stuff of daily life – food, drink, clothing, shelter – to a kind of art.

A Florentine leather craftsman deep in concentration

SNAPSHOTS

ACCOMMODATION

Sleeping in central Florence can be a competitive sport. Prices are high, and the city is booked solid during holiday weekends, especially around Christmas, Easter and 1 May. Plan as far ahead as possible at these times, and indeed anytime from April to June and also September to mid-November.

Florence offers sweet sleeps in all price ranges and any central neighbourhood is convenient to virtually all the major sights. That said, Santa Croce puts you within crawling distance of the city's major nightlife hub. The Oltrarno offers a degree of removal from the crowds. East of Santa Maria Novella train station, San Lorenzo offers the greatest number of options but also crowded streets and tourist-targeted bad pasta joints and overpriced internet cafes. High-end sleeps, by contrast, tend to be clustered around Piazza della Repubblica and along the Arno. At this range, you can choose between cool minimalism, period Renaissance palazzi, or grand 19th-century affairs. For panoramic views and country charms, head up to Fiesole, a half-hour commute to the city centre.

If on a budget, there are decent options distributed throughout the city, from workable hostels to a number of charming if threadbare *pensioni* (guesthouses) that offer some kind of differential. Pluses range from city views and Renaissance appointments to kindly Anglo matrons. Just be aware that you may have to give up a private bathroom, air con (a big sacrifice in summer) and/or a degree of quiet in the process.

Florence is cultivating an expanding crop of B&Bs, also called *affitacamere*, from lace-doily cheapies with a crucifix over every bed to refined *residenze d'epoca* (historical residences) done up in period furnishings.

Less interesting is the city's midrange, two- to three-star options. They tend to be surprisingly kitschy and threadbare, given prices that would be at the high end in many destinations. But they have air-con, private loos and a degree of quiet.

At the budget end, expect to pay between €60 to €120 for a double room. Midrange doubles range from €120 to €250, while four-and five-star affairs start at around €300 per night and go way up from there.

When reserving a room, make sure you ask for a *camera matrimoniale* if you're after a double bed, or a *camera doppia* if you want twin beds.

WEB RESOURCES

Promhotels (www.promhotels.it) specialises in Florentine hotels, with online bookings in all price ranges. As its name suggests **Family Hotels & Restaurants** (www.familyhotels.it) offers bookings at family-run establishments in Florence and across Tuscany. While a global site, **Venere** (www.venere.com) is worth checking out for promotional rates. Finally, the **Associazione Bed & Breakfast Affitacamere** (www.abba-firenze.it) is a good one-stop shop for B&Bs.

BEST FOR ROOMS WITH VIEWS
> Continentale (www.lungarnohotels.com) Arno and Ponte Vecchio
> Gallery Hotel Art (www.lungarnohotels.com) Arno and Ponte Vecchio
> Il Salotto di Firenze (www.ilsalottodifirenze.it) Duomo
> Villa Aurora, Fiesole (www.villaaurora.net) Florence panorama
> Villa San Michele (www.villasanmichele.orient-express.com) Florence panorama

BEST FOR SLEEPING WITH HISTORY
> Hotel La Scaletta (www.hotellascaletta.it)
> Hotel Morandi all Crocetta (www.hotelmorandi.it)

> Hotel Scoti (www.hotelscoti.com)
> Palazzo Magnani Ferroni (www.florencepalace.com)
> Relais Santa Croce (www.relaisantacroce.com)

BEST FOR...
> A Zenlike retreat – Hotel Cestelli (www.hotelcestelli.com)
> A scene out of EM Forster – Hotel Scoti (www.hotelscoti.com)
> Shamelessly palatial living – Palazzo Magnani Feroni (www.palazzomagnaniferoni.com)
> Rooms with fine views – Continentale (www.lungarnohotels.com)
> Worldly pleasures in a monastic setting – Hotel Morandi all Crocetta (www.hotelmorandi.it)

MUSEUMS & GALLERIES

Possessing as it does 'the greatest concentration of universally renowned works of art in the world' – if you doubt our claim, just ask Unesco – it hardly needs saying that Florence's museums are, yes, jaw-droppingly good.

Everyone, of course, thinks immediately of the Uffizi (p45), and rightly so. It's a true showstopper, with its Giottos and Giorgiones, Da Vincis and Lippis. While it can be arduous going, with its small rooms and large queues, the collection remains serenely peerless. Just across the Arno, the Palazzo Pitti (p114) is a kind of mini-Louvre that shelters everything from carriages to Caravaggios. Though quality is more variable than at the perfectionist Uffizi, it's a great ramble filled with stunning surprises. Completing the triumvirate is the Galleria dell'Accademia (p87), a one-hit wonder with its middling collection of paintings (by Florentine standards, anyway) and Michelangelo's knockout version of *David*.

The city's second-tier museums would be first-tier anywhere else. The Museo del Bargello (p97) is possibly the city's least-appreciated treasure house, with a collection that ranges from Michelangelo's sensual *Drunken Bacchus* to the delicate, and quintessentially Florentine, ceramic statuary of the della Robbia family. At the Museo di San Marco (p89), you'll understand why the monastery's most illustrious resident, painter Fra Angelico, was nicknamed Beato (Blessed). His panels and frescoes possess both riotous joy and otherworldly beauty. Finally, the Museo dell'Opera del Duomo (p45) hoards extraordinary treasures from the adjacent Duomo, including works by Ghiberti, Donatello and Michelangelo.

The city is also packed with smaller museums that are as much about the buildings themselves as the collections they house. The mazelike Palazzo Vecchio (p48) provides insight into the internecine struggles on which Florentine history was built. The fortified elegance of Palazzo Strozzi (p48) and Palazzo Medici-Riccardi (p78) give us a peak into the life of two wealthy Renaissance banking families. And the Palazzo Davanzati (p46) does the same for their medieval equivalent.

Finally, the city's smaller museums have their own quirky stories to tell. Take the quaintly elegant Museo dell'Opificio delle Pietre Dure (p89), devoted to a peculiarly Florentine form of mosaic made of marble and semiprecious stones that have been fitted together with inconceivable precision. Though poorly curated, the nearby Museo Archeologico (p88) possesses a first-rate jumble of Etruscan art and artefacts. The new Alinari National Photography Museum (p63) is the latest of the pint-sized powers, with its creative displays of photography from its 19th-century beginnings through to the present. The melancholic little Museo di Firenze com'Era (p99) tells the city's history through paintings, artefacts and scale models. Finally, the macabre Museo Zoologico La Specola (p113) reveals the gory details about our innards with shockingly realistic wax versions of human bodies in various states of autopsy.

Not enough for you? We hope not, because these options don't even include the city's offerings of art in situ (p162).

BEST FOR RENAISSANCE LOOT
> Galleria degli Uffizi (p45)
> Galleria dell'Accademia (p87)
> Museo del Bargello (p97)
> Museo di San Marco (p89)
> Palazzo Pitti (p114)

BEST FOR...
> Shock value – Museo Zoologico La Specola (p113)
> Shoe fetishists – Museo Ferragamo (p46)
> The privileged few – Corrodio Vasariano (p48)
> Male nudes – Museo del Bargello (p97)
> Helpful signage – Museo dell'Opera del Duomo (p45)

Above The Galleria degli Uffizi houses the gems of the Renaissance

SNAPSHOTS

SHOPPING

While Florentines have long been crack craftspeople, salesmanship is not their historical strength. That's changing fast as the bijou city remakes itself into a shopper's haven. But we're not talking the Wal-Mart model. More like Avenue Montaigne.

It seems all the world's luxury brands have come to roost in Via de' Tornabuoni. It's long been a fashionable thoroughfare, but sometime in the early 1990s an MBA in Milan must have done a study of foot traffic and discovered the potential goldmine. Over the last decade or so, ground floors of palazzo after palazzo have been transformed into shimmering temples of fashion. You can find everyone from Prada to Cartier, but we're rooting for hometown players such as Gucci, Cavalli and Ferragamo, all of whom have large stores here. As Tornabuoni retail maxes out, smart shops have sprung up along neighbouring Via della Vigna Nuova.

However, Tornabuoni reveals only the glitzy tip of the iceberg. By our lights, the most interesting finds reside in far more discreet shops, many of which double as workshops where artisans hammer out one-of-a-kind creations. Don't expect bargains, exactly, but at least you'll come away with something that your neighbours lack. Over the centuries, the city that made its first fortune on fabrics has perfected an admirably wide range of handmade crafts, including ceramics, gold, paper and book-binding, intricate marble mosaics, and leatherwork of every kind, including exquisite shoes, gloves, coats and bags.

The Oltrarno neighbourhood (p122) has for centuries been the natural home of Florentine artisans. See world-renowned jeweller Angela Caputi (p126) at work in her immaculate atelier. Or breathe in a little dust kicked up from the sawing and sanding at Francesco di Firenze (p128). Also in the Oltrarno, Borgo San Jacopo and Via Santo Spirito are streets that offer more avant-garde versions of the upscale wares found along Tornabuoni, such as the handmade duds at Quelle Tre (p129) or the carefully curated selection of emerging fashion at A Piedi Nudi nel Parco (p126).

In Tuscany, even farming has been raised to an art, and shops around Florence bring you the finest from its fields, orchards, pastures and vineyards. At shops such as Olio & Convivium (p135), regional foodstuffs come in tasteful, gift-ready packages. You also can buy Chianti direct from the source, for example at Cantinetta dei Verrazzano (p52). Or head to Mercato Centrale (p82) for a great hunk of pecorino (a mild cheese made from sheep's milk) or smoked boar wrapped in plain brown paper.

If you want your own piece of the Renaissance, the high-end antique dealers along the Oltrarno's Via Maggio will oblige. Or if you prefer to wear a bit of history, check out high-end vintage at Elio Ferraro (p64). At the other end of the scale, the street stalls around Mercato Centrale (p82) hawk second-rate if largely acceptable versions of Florentine crafts.

Finally, Florence offers some truly fine one-off establishments. San Jacopo Show (p130) specialises in handmade mannequins. You can buy your stationery from the purveyors to Napoleon at Pineider (p51). The grandest of all, though, is Officina Profumo-Farmaceutica di Santa Maria Novella (p65), a privately owned spin-off of the adjoining monastery. Its soaps, scents and original 17th-century baroque interior are a feast for the senses.

BEST FOR ONE-OF-A-KIND FINDS
> Angela Caputi (p50)
> Elio Ferraro (p64)
> Mercato dei Pulci (p100)
> Officina Profumo-Farmaceutica di Santa Maria Novella (p65)
> San Jacopo Show (p130)

BEST FOR LOCAL CRAFTS
> Paper – Giulio Giannini & Figlio (p128)
> Leather – MM (p129)
> Ceramics – Sbigoli Terrecote (p100)
> Handmade shoes – Stefano Bemer (p130)
> Jewellery – Angela Caputi (p126)

Top left You'll find plenty of style inspiration in the boutiques of Florence

ARCHITECTURE

Both revolutionary and arrestingly beautiful, Brunelleschi's cathedral dome (p12) still dominates the Florentine skyline after nearly six centuries. It gives form to a city that was itself on the rise, that dared to innovate, and was in the process of encompassing what became the Renaissance.

However, the city's architectural roots reach much deeper into the past, in fact all the way to the Roman world Brunelleschi himself was trying to resurrect. Roman city planning is still evident in the neat grid of streets between the Duomo and the Piazza della Signoria, and under them lie long-buried baths, temples and domestic dwellings. Little remains of the period between the ancient era and Florence's rise to prominence in the late Middle Ages, a rare exception being the rough, round Torre della Pagliazza (p50), believed to be a 6th-century Byzantine structure.

The city's rising fortunes are evident in a series of Romanesque structures that, like Brunelleschi's dome, also recall the city's Roman roots. In fact, the Battistero (Baptistery; p41), with its round arches and classical columns, fooled generations of Florentines into believing it was in fact a Roman temple, though in fact it probably dates to the 11th century. San Miniato al Monte (p109) is the city's other Romanesque masterpiece. Medieval towers from this period still dot the city, including Torre della Castagna (p50).

By the 14th century, the city had turned itself into an economic power-house of bankers and cloth-makers. Gothic architecture, with its pointed arches and profusion of detail, had swept across Europe, and the city built what remain its greatest churches in that style, including Santa Maria Novella, Santa Croce and the nave of the Duomo (p12). However, its massive civic buildings, including the Palazzo Vecchio (p48) and Museo del Bargello (p97), are in some ways more impressive. Their sheer size reveal the city's growing self-confidence, though they retain a military bearing during a time when war and civil strife were a constant threat.

By the 15th century, the Medici family had brought the fractious city a semblance of order. The resulting peace and prosperity spurred architects to invent an architectural idiom for what was an unprecedented political construction – an independent, prosperous, and vaguely democratic city-state with imperial ambitions. Roman and Greek models were, of course, an obvious fit, helped out by the growing cult among the intellectuals of the time for all things classical. Brunelleschi's dome is the greatest example of this very early Renaissance period, but equally revolutionary in a way are Alberti's facade of Santa Maria Novella (p59) and his Palazzo Rucellai (p63). Meanwhile, Brunelleschi continued to refine his art on projects such as San Lorenzo (p73), Santo Spirito (p123), and Spedale degli Innocenti (p90), all of which borrow classical motifs but achieve a combination of balance, order and simplicity that are uniquely Florentine.

By the 16th century, Florence's fortunes were waning, leaving little money for new construction. As a result the city centre looks much like it did in 1550. Still, it does have several fine examples of the flamboyant late phase of the Renaissance known as mannerism: the Galleria degli Uffizi (p45) and Michelangelo's ground-breaking work in San Lorenzo (p73), plus a smattering of 17th-century baroque works such as Chiesa di Ognissanti (p62).

The city centre did undergo some major changes in the late 19th century, when it lost its medieval city walls and gained the overblown, neo-classical Piazza della Repubblica (p49), which was carved out of the dense maze of medieval streets. Still, architects have tended to remain faithful to the city's golden age in the 1400s, preserving the sense of rigor, order and simplicity that still define its melancholic beauty today.

BEST REVOLUTIONARY STRUCTURES
> Biblioteca Medicea-Laurenziana (p76)
> Brunelleschi's dome (p12)
> Cappelle Medicee (p77)
> Facade of Santa Maria Novella (p59)
> Palazzo Rucellai (p63)
> Spedale degli Innocenti (p90)

BEST UNDERAPPRECIATED MASTERPIECES
> Battistero (p41)
> Museo del Bargello (p97)
> Palazzo Rucellai (p63)
> Ponte Santa Trínita (p63)
> San Miniato al Monte (p109)

Above Leon Battista Alberti's magnificent facade to the Basilica di Santa Maria Novella (p59)

FOOD

There's no question that you can eat like a king in the capital of Tuscany. But in a city that attracts nearly 10 million tourists a year, you can also pay regal prices for even cafeteria-quality fare. For the finicky foodie, advance research is required.

The secret ingredient of Tuscan food is, well, the ingredients. Tuscan husbandry is justly famous, with many farmers still tending their pigs and cows, olives and grapes with the pride of artisans. Head to Mercato Centrale (p82) to see the products of their labour. Artisanal cheeses, especially pecorino as well as *salumi* (cured meats) such as the gamey *salsiccia di cingale* (wild-boar sausage) make a meal in themselves. And in autumn, truffles (p22) fresh from the Tuscan earth appear in shops around the city. It's understandable why the Tuscan cook considers it a duty not to transform ingredients but merely to reveal their innate glory. Even the typical bread, *pane toscana*, is made without salt, providing as pure as possible a grounding for the palette.

Nor is creativity a goal in itself. The idea, rather, is to take classic recipes such as *ribollito* (bean and bread soup) or *bistecca alla fiorentina* (p21) and make them sing. As Tuscans put it, 'To cook like your mother is good, to cook like your grandmother is better.'

Just mention Tuscan food in London and New York and you conjure full-colour magazine spreads and food snobbery. But Tuscan food is essentially peasant fare. In fact, the rest of Italy calls the Tuscans *mangia-fagioli* (bean-eaters) because of their culinary frugality. Stale bread is recycled into soup, while cow's lung, if not exactly a delicacy, is a perfectly respectable option. And gourmands here seem to know all the names of the various parts of the bovine intestines, each appreciated for its own taste and texture.

Fortunately, there are plenty of places that haven't been tainted by tourist euros, from humble tripe stands all the way up to three-starred Enoteca Pinchiorri (p102). Top-flight sandwich shops oblige small budgets and tight schedules. There are still a few good-value old-fashioned eateries starring *nonna* in the kitchen, *mamma* at the register, and a pair of 20-something grandchildren serving the tables with a sometimes-surly reticence. A smattering of excellent pizzerias, offering both the thin-crusted Tuscan and the thicker Neapolitan style, please all comers.

Finally, there are the expensive *ristoranti*, with their white tablecloths and exquisite versions of classic Tuscan dishes and, increasingly, more modern, colourful versions of the same. The best of them make the palate sing.

A good general rule, though, is either to pay very little for your food, or quite a lot. Why? Because the middle range has realised that, with a constantly fresh crop of tourists, quantity is more profitable rather than quality. They're not bad, exactly, and some of them serve up a fine atmosphere, such as fine terrace seating or vaulted Renaissance ceilings. But they won't make you swoon, which, if you've come all the way to Tuscany, really should be the case.

Portions in Italy tend to be small because you're expected (though not required) to order two courses. The *primo* (first course) is generally pasta or soup, followed by a *segundo* (main course) that often consists of grilled or stewed meat with a *contorno* (a side dish, sauteed or roasted vegetables). To these you may add an antipasto, such as a plate of olives or local cheese and meats, to begin. *Dolci* (desserts) are often simple, such as *panna cotta* (cooked cream) or stewed fruit. Or you can skip dessert and head instead to the nearest great *gelateria* (ice cream shop). Every neighbourhood has its excellent exemplar.

BEST CREATIVE TUSCAN
> Borgo San Jacopo (p131)
> Enoteca Pinchiorri (p102)
> Ora d'Aria (p102)
> Ristorante Cibrèo (p103)
> Ristorante Pane e Vino (p135)

BEST GELATO
> Carabè (p90)
> Gelateria Santa Trinita (p133)
> Grom (p53)
> Vestri (p105)
> Vivoli (p105)

BEST QUICK & CHEAP
> Amon (p66)
> Gastronomia Giuliano (p102)
> I Fratellini (p54)
> Oil Shoppe (p91)
> Pizzaria Gustavino (p53)

BEST HOME-STYLE TUSCAN
> Nerbone (p82)
> Da Ruggero (p116)
> Sabatino (p136)
> Da Camillo (p133)

ART IN SITU

There is a palpable difference between looking at an altarpiece in a gallery and seeing it on the actual altar for which it was created. There, the rich hues and dramatic narrative take on a new power. And in Florence, where you often seem to be hustled past masterpieces in museums, seeking individual works in situ can provide rare moments of calm and intimacy.

Opportunities to see art in situ are many. Some, such as Masaccio's fantastic frescoes in Cappella Brancacci (p123) and Benozzo Gozzoli's Cappella dei Magi (p76), do attract big crowds in small spaces. Others, though, you may get all to yourself, such as Andrea del Castango's *Last Supper,* with its vicious-looking Judas and disturbingly vivid palette, in Sant'Apollonia (p78). In fact, Last Supper frescoes were a Florentine speciality, and you can see versions in *cenacoli* (monastic dining rooms) around the city.

Some pieces are exposed to the elements, though they may be excellent replicas, such as Ghiberti's *Gates of Paradise* on the Battistero (p41) and *David* in front of the Uffizi. The Loggia dei Lanzi, by contrast, (p49) shelters a tumult of original statuary, including works by Cellini and Giambologna.

BEST LAST SUPPER FRESCOES
> Cenacolo di Fuligno (p78)
> Cenacolo di Ognissanti (p62)
> Museo di San Marco (p89)
> Cenacolo di Sant'Apollonia (p78)

BEST OVERLOOKED WORKS
> Andrea del Sarto's fresco cycle in the Chiostro dello Scalzo (p86)
> Ghirlandaio's fresco cycle in Santa Trínita (p59)
> *Last Judgment* in the Battistero (p41)
> Paolo Uccello's frescoes in the Chiostri di Santa Maria Novella (p63)
> Pontormo's *Deposition* in Santa Felicità (p109)
> *Last Judgment* in the Duomo (p44)
> The ceiling at the Spedale degli Innocenti (p90; see photo at right)

CAFFÈ SOCIETY

Like the coffee itself, the Florentine cafe scene is frothy, bracing and richly nuanced. There are the high-class numbers, such as clubby, wood-panelled Procacci (p56) and the art nouveau splendours of Gilli (p55). There are the Bohemian options such as the rustic Caffè degli Artigiani (p131; see photo below) and the lively, literary Libreria Café la Cité (p137), both in the Oltrarno. There are those that provide ringside seats amid the tumult and beauty of the city's best piazzas, such as Rivoire (p54) and Ristorante Ricchi (p135). Finally there are those geared to aficionados whose focus is on the bean itself, such as Chiaroscuro (p55) and Caffellatte (p90).

You can take your coffee in two ways. Join the locals standing amid the hiss and steam of the bar, where prices are low and service is brisk. When your espresso arrives, stir in some sugar, swirl it a few times to take off the burn, then down it in a sip or two before heading off. Even the most elegant addresses offer this utilitarian option. Or, for two or three times more euros, you can sit for an hour or two on the strength of a single drink.

BEST FOR...

> Panoramic views – Rooftop *caffè* at La Rinascente (p50)
> Literary ghosts – Giubbe Rosse (p55)
> High-minded flirting – Libreria Café la Cité (p137)
> Sweet tooths – Nannini Coffee Shop (p82)
> Fashionistas – Giacosa Roberto Cavalli (p69)

FLORENCE AFTER DARK

For a mid-sized, provincial city, Florence's nightlife packs a mean little punch. Certainly it's bustling, which makes sense considering all the students, tourists and other lucky bastards who don't have to set an alarm. Then there's the Italians' natural affability, the lack of 'open container' laws (ie you can drink in public places) and temperate weather.

For Florentines, night begins around dusk with *aperitivi* (pre-dinner drinks) from about 7pm to 10pm, when many bars offer a free buffet with the drink (p56). Weather permitting, people may then head for their local piazza to meet friends, drink more, and discuss strategies for the evening. At midnight, it's time to consider clubbing, which can range from the cosily decadent Montecarla Club (p119) to the mainstream Central Park (p70). When funds are limited, a church step and bottle of wine make an evening.

To sniff out the Bohemian party, head to Piazza Santo Spirito. If your taste runs to Americans studying abroad, there's Via de' Benci and nearby Piazza Santa Croce. For upscale 30- and 40-somethings, check out Piazza Nicola Demidoff as well as the riverside spots further east.

Firenze Spettacolo, a small weekly publication, provides events listings (also at www.firenzespettacolo.it). For ticketed events, try Box Office (p70).

BEST ENTERTAINMENT

> Clubbing – Central Park (p70)
> Underground gay scene – Tabasco Disco Gay (p57)
> Hip-hop – YAB on a Monday (p57)
> Dressing the part – La Dolce Vita (p136)
> Mosh pits – Montecarla Club (p119)

BEST APERITIVI

> Fusion Bar (p52)
> Negroni (p118; see photo above)
> Noir (p69)
> Rex Cafe (p92)
> Sky Lounge (p56)

PARKS & GARDENS

With no green space and hardly even a tree, central Florence can feel like a relentless, if highly evolved, urban jungle. Add the fact that navigating its streets requires frequent plunges into traffic, as footpaths are too narrow to accommodate locals, let alone tour groups. Fortunately grass, trees and a bit of elbowroom are never more than a brisk, 15-minute walk away.

The most obvious escape is up into the Giardino di Boboli (p112), with their formal axes, Baroque fountains and shady footpaths. To feel like you have a piece of them to yourself, head into the maze of paths that branch off from its long, cypress-lined alley. Nearby, the Giardino di Bardini (p109) is a manicured wonder, with a baroque stairway, English-style gardens, and incomparable views across Florence. If legs allow, combine the gardens with the wonderful, countrylike hike up to San Miniato al Monte (p109).

At the northern edge of the centre, the Giardino dei Semplici (p87) was founded as a medicinal garden in the 16th century. Today its greenhouse is fragrant with citrus blossoms, while its 2.3 hectares outdoors are devoted to medicinal plants, Tuscan spices, and wildflowers from the Apennines.

Heading west along the Arno to the sprawling, wooded Parco delle Cascine (p63) offers 160 hectares of trees, lawns and trails. For longer hikes, investigate the Anello del Rinascimento (Renaissance Ring), a 170km ring of trails that circles Florence, with Fiesole as its jumping-off point (p140).

Experience the tranquillity of the Giardino di Bardini as the Medici would have done during the Renaissance

VIEWS

Standing on the ramparts of the Forte di Belvedere (p109), you grasp what motivated Florentines to reintroduce the third dimension into Western art. The land itself conspires, with its cunning combination of lovely green hills, wide valley expanses and framing blue peaks. At the same time, the vast Duomo imposes its serene, humanising order upon the scene.

Even if your room lacks a view, the rest of the city offers up a stunning array, from the intimate to the panoramic. A cool drink in the shade of Piazza Santo Spirito provides a close-up of Oltrarno's street life, framed by tree-lined palazzi and the negative space of an unfinished church facade. Or you can head up to hilltop Fiesole (p140), whose commanding heights take in the panorama of greater Florence in a single sweep.

The hilly southern banks of the Arno deliver their own remarkable series of city vistas. Besides the Forte di Belvedere, there are the heights of the Giardino di Boboli (p112), the steps of San Miniato (p109) and, most remarkable of all, the steep slopes of the Giardino di Bardini (p109; see photo below), which seem to hover just above the city's lovely rooftops.

Not for the claustrophobic, the 463 steps to the top of the Duomo (p12) offers the best of the manmade vistas, though some swear by the adjacent Campanile (p44), as from there you can see Brunelleschi's dome.

BEST VIEWS
> Vast panoramas – Fiesole's Via San Francesco (p140)
> Close-up of the Duomo – Campanile (p44)
> 360-degree city views – Top of the Duomo's dome (p12)
> Country prospects inside the city limits – San Miniato al Monte (p109)

>BACKGROUND

Seeking out Tuscan treats inside the city's Mercato Centrale (p82)

BACKGROUND

HISTORY

Its urban core may be stubbornly pre-Modern, but Florence today is a prosperous, forward-looking, middle-sized European city. It still makes the lion's share of its living off its glory days, with tourism its single biggest industry. However, the economy also gets a solid contribution from industry, from fine textiles to compressors and pharmaceuticals. With a metropolitan population approaching 1 million, Florence is for the first time attracting non-Italian immigrants, with an estimated 60,000 foreign-born residents, mostly Chinese, Filipinos, Africans and Eastern Europeans.

A CITY FLOURISHES

After conquering Gaul, Julius Caesar founded Florentia (the Flourishing One) in 59 BC to protect the land route to his new colony. The outlines of that original military settlement are still visible in the grid of streets between the Duomo and Piazza della Signoria. However, the history of nearby Fiesole, founded by Etruscans, reaches back to at least the 7th century BC. The Etruscans defended their city fiercely against Roman incursions in the 3rd century BC, though eventually they capitulated.

It's easy to understand why the Etruscans fought for their ancestral land, with its agriculturally rich valleys, productive mines and quarries, hillsides conducive to grapes and olives, and mountains that yielded lumber and their favourite form of protein – wild boar. In short, it represented a small but self-sufficient little universe unto itself – much the way Tuscany likes to imagine itself down to today.

FROM PAGAN ROME TO HOLY ROME

During the 2nd and 3rd centuries AD, Roman Florence became a prosperous little river port. By the 4th century, the empire began to weaken even as Christianity was on the rise. Florence probably got its first two churches, San Lorenzo (p73) and Santa Felicità (p109) during this period, though both have since been entirely rebuilt.

As the empire crumbled over the next centuries, Tuscany was overrun in turn by Goths and Lombards. A modicum of order was established when Charlemagne swept through Italy in the 8th century AD, establishing the Holy Roman Empire and making nearby Lucca the regional capital.

A MEDIEVAL POWERHOUSE

In around 1000 AD, the rulers in Lucca decided to move their headquarters to Florence. Then in 1115, Countess Matilda granted the growing city its independence. Supported by its textile industry, Florence began to assert itself as a regional power, first conquering Fiesole in the late 12th century.

For the next three centuries, the little republic was run by the city's merchants and bankers, who began to organize powerful *arti* (guilds) to promote their interests. The Museo del Bargello (p97) and Palazzo Vecchio (p48) still serve as impressive reminders of the city's growing fortunes.

Disaster came in 1348, when the Black Death wiped out half the city's population. However, Florence's neighbours suffered similarly, so the city's rising prominence was not checked. But the sudden shortage of workers did encourage organisation among the labour classes. In 1378 the *ciompi* (wool carders) led a short-lived insurrection, forming a government that represented all social classes. However, the rich merchants were back in the saddle after a matter of months.

Meanwhile, the city's growing wealth enabled its gradual takeover of Tuscany. The biggest prize was Pisa, which it conquered in 1406. A few decades later, the confident little city hired Brunelleschi to build the largest dome since ancient times (p12) launching a cultural and artistic sea-change that would become known as the Renaissance (p172).

THE RISE OF THE MEDICI

While theoretically still a republic, Florence gradually came under the sway of a single family over the course of the 15th century. During the 1420s, Cosimo de' Medici (p76), known as Cosimo il Vecchio and founder of the dynasty, began forming alliances with the city's smaller guilds against the city's oligarchs. Eventually he found himself in prison, but upon his release, he won the general confidence of the public by neutralising an even greater threat – the powerful Sforza family of Milan. Ever a cunning diplomat, he did so by establishing a favourable alliance rather than force. A great patron of the arts, Cosimo also turned Florence into a pre-eminent cultural centre. His descendents maintained the family tradition, especially his grandson Lorenzo the Magnificent in the late 15th century.

After several periods of exile, including a brief rule by ascetic monk Savonarola (see boxed text, p86), the Medicis were installed as dukes in

1530. They managed to buy Siena from Austria in 1557, marking the high-point of the city's political fortunes, though trouble was in the wind.

A BACKWATER BECOMES A CAPITAL

Throughout the 16th century, Florence's control of the wool and banking markets were subject to increasing competition. The biggest blow came in the 1630s, when prices for its woollen goods collapsed. The capital of the Renaissance rapidly reverted to a quaint backwater.

Fortunes changed when Florence was chosen as the capital of the newly united Italian nation in 1865. The city's historic core, which had changed little since the 16th century, was partially modernised (p115). However, Rome quickly stole Florentine glory and the capital moved south in 1870.

Without a clear future, the city learned to capitalise on its past when, in the second half of the 19th century, train travel brought the city within reach of a new class of tourists.

20TH-CENTURY FLORENCE

The city stayed quietly distant from history until WWII, when retreating Nazis razed its ancient bridges (except Ponte Vecchio), and bombs destroyed a portion of its medieval fabric.

After the war, rapid industrialisation turned Florence into Italy's third-largest industrial centre. It also became a hotbed of fashion, thanks to postwar designers such as Guccio Gucci and Salvatore Ferragamo, who created showy luxuries for a new breed of Italian capitalists.

Rapid industrialisation also resulted in a new class of working-class wage earners who streamed in from the Tuscan countryside. They, together with the city's intellectuals, helped make the city a stronghold of the Italian left, which it remains to this day.

LIFE AS A FLORENTINE

THE GOOD LIFE, FLORENTINE-STYLE

Florence may be a communist hotbed, but its residents never adopted the kind of Calvinistic distrust of pleasure that runs through the northern European left. A visit to the bars of the Bohemian Oltrarno district will reveal that a sense of personal style, even if achieved on the cheap, is a kind of universal Florentine right.

Likewise, residents of all political persuasions are united in considering great food a given feature of the good life. Eating is the nucleus of virtually

ME, COMPLAIN?

Is life hard for the typical Florentine? Chances are, they'll tell you it is. And they have their reasons. Rents in the city centre have skyrocketed in recent years, but salaries have not. Public projects, including the city's new tramlines (p71), are invariably mired in controversy and subject to interminable delays. There are complaints about corruption at the highest levels, though a Florentine will quickly distinguish their brand as far more civilized than that of, say, Naples or Palermo. Eight million tourists bring jobs and money, but everyone says they spend too little, since most just come for an afternoon. And of course they also clog the streets, tax the infrastructure and, worst of all, help water down good restaurants with their undiscerning palates.

At the same time, good Florentines wouldn't dream of moving. Like most Italians, they identify far more with their city and region than their nation. They may roll their eyes at the newcomer's awe in the face of Renaissance monuments, but are jealously proud of them too. And they may complain about prices, but in a city that still places the highest value on aesthetics, they all seem perfectly able to scrounge enough for a slick jacket, scarf and shoes to maintain their *bella figura* (good public face).

every social interaction. Even when not eating, they are talking about eating – which *forno* (bakery) has the best bread, which greengrocer passes off rotten onions, which restaurants have not yet been ruined by tourists. A home-cooked meal still forms the backbone of an evening out, even for the younger generation. And not just because prices in Florentine restaurants outstrip salaries, but also because they feel they can usually eat better at home anyway. And anyway, it's just more convivial.

Because central Florence is so small, Florentines are constantly running into their friends. An evening out is as close as the neighbourhood piazza, where there is never a cover charge. And unlike, say, the British Isles, evening plans tend to involve less alcohol and more conversation that is actually coherent. Polemics, whether about Trotsky or truffles, is considered high sport.

Escaping Florence is the final ingredient of the Florentine good life. The summer heat is oppressive, and the city heads en masse to the Mediterranean coast. And if a Florentine doesn't have a house in the Tuscan countryside, a friend surely will. In fact, the frequent intercourse between city and country has been part of the Florentine life since at least Renaissance times. When returning home, it is vital to come with fresh rural bounty: a superior pecorino (cheese made from sheep milk), wild asparagus, apricots picked that very afternoon.

A COOL RECEPTION

If you imagine Italians as ebullient and emotional people who are constantly laughing, crying, and cajoling you into eating more pasta, you may be disappointed by the cool reception that awaits you in Florence. It's understandable to a certain extent. If you were a shopkeeper, how many times would you want to give directions in a language not your own to strangers who won't even be buying bottled water?

If you feel slighted, consider that even other Tuscans complain that the Florentines are clannish and aloof. Perhaps it's their pride in past glories. Perhaps it's their historic distrust of outsiders in a land in which one's neighbour and ally – Pisa, Siena, Rome, Milan – could quickly turn mortal enemy. Or perhaps the clannishness has its source in the city itself, which for centuries was both wealthy and subject to rapidly shifting alliance and deadly vendettas. Under such conditions, you too would want to hold your cards close.

THE RENAISSANCE: A BRIEF INTRO

Literally meaning rebirth, the Renaissance is generally defined as the rediscovery of Roman and Greek learning together with a rejection of rigid doctrine in favour of a 'humanistic' philosophy that emphasised intellectual curiosity and human experience over purely written knowledge. In this vein, Renaissance artists looked closely at, and attempted to recreate, the natural world. Gilded halos disappeared, saints gained naturalistic human bodies, and space deepened to include a third dimension. At the same time, artists, long limited to religious themes, began to depict classical subjects as well as present scenes from contemporary life.

WHY FLORENCE?

There are many reasons why Florence became the nexus for these developments. It was among Europe's wealthiest cities, solving the simple problem of funding. With business interests throughout Europe and beyond, the city was also constantly exposed to diverse cultures, preparing the ground for new concepts and ways of thinking.

In addition, the Roman past was never very far away. Rome itself might seem the stronger candidate, but as the seat of the Church, it was naturally more conservative. Meanwhile, in a continent dominated by feudal aristocrats, Florence's dynamic ruling class could not justify their rule by noble birth and turned to the republican traditions of ancient Rome as a way to validate their quasi-democratic oligarchy.

Finally, Florence had long made its fortune creating beautiful textiles, resulting in both a profound respect for aesthetics as well as a large body of skilled artisans.

MEDIEVAL FORERUNNERS

Traditionally the Renaissance has been characterised as a clean break with the Middle Ages, though increasingly historians see it as the continuation of developments already underway. The works of Dante (c 1265–1321; p52) and Petrarch (c 1304–74) are prime literary examples. Ciambue (c 1240–1302), considered the last of the great Byzantine-style painters, was already adopting a more naturalistic style. His great pupil Giotto (c 1267–1337) made great advances towards naturalistic forms and three-dimensional space, always beautifully but sometimes awkwardly.

EARLY RENAISSANCE

The dome (p44) of Brunelleschi (1377–1446) is recognised as the first great work of Renaissance architecture. However, his Basilica di San Lorenzo (p73) and Spedale degli Innocenti (p90) more clearly demonstrate the order, geometry and classical motifs that define the early Renaissance.

Brunelleschi also helped theorize three-dimensional perspective, along with writer and architect Leon Battista Alberti (1404–72). The frescos of Masaccio (1401–28) in Santa Maria Novella (p59) and the Cappella Brancacci (p123) make good on their theories, and are considered the first truly Renaissance paintings. Other great works of this period include Lorenzo Ghiberti's doors for the Battistero (p41) and Donatello's *David* in the Bargello (p97). Meanwhile, the great Fra Angelico (c 1395–1455; p89) was marrying medieval and Renaissance currents into a uniquely beautiful hybrid.

HIGH RENAISSANCE

During the period roughly from 1450 to 1520, known as the High Renaissance, Florentine artists were funded largely by the Medici family – a sea change, since the Church had long been Europe's almost sole patron. Like the Church, the Medici used art to glorify and justify their dominance.

BOOKS & FILMS

For a general introduction to Italian culture, Luigi Barzini's *The Italians* is a must. Some of the facts are dated, but the general principles are still incisive, entertaining and spot on. More recently, *The Dark Heart of Italy*, by Tobias Jones, provides an excellent general introduction to contemporary Italy.

For a general portrait of Florence's culture and art, you can't beat Mary McCarthy's *The Stones of Florence*. It is a work of literature as well as a witty portrait of the city that, though written in the 1950s, still remains highly trenchant. Christopher Hibbert's *Florence* is another highly readable history of the city and its major figures.

For deeper investigations into particular topics, consider Frederick Hartt's sweeping classic *The History of Italian Renaissance Art*. Another compulsively readable work is Ross King's *Brunelleschi's Dome: The Story of the Great Cathedral*.

Of course there are also the works of Florentines themselves. Dante's *Divine Comedy* takes place in Heaven and Hell, but the characters are largely his Florentine comrades. Boccaccio's *Decameron* documents 14th-century Florence life. Machiavelli's *The Prince* is a classic of political theory and a window into the dangers faced by Italian Renaissance rulers. And Giorgio Vasari's *The Lives of the Artists* charts the course of the Renaissance and the lives of its greatest artists.

A Room with a View, both EM Forester's 1908 novel as well as the 1985 film version, use Florence as the splendid backdrop to tell the moving and witty story of a young woman's coming of age. *Tea with Mussolini* (1998) is set in the city's quirky British expat community as it comes to terms with Mussolini's rule.

Leading figures of the period include Sandro Botticelli (1445–1510) and Domenico Ghirlandaio (1449–94), both known for the sweetness and harmony of their works.

However, two artists emerged to push the envelope much further. The rigorous Leonardo da Vinci (1452–1519) based his art on the scientific study of the natural world, including the ability to capture the 'smoky' atmospherics of three-dimensional space. And his chiaroscuro technique also led to more realistic modelling of forms by relying on light and shade. Meanwhile Michelangelo (1475–1564) brought a new immediacy and dramatic power to his depiction of the human form and human emotions.

A combination of political chaos and papal patronage wrested both these great artists away from Florence in the early 1500s. Soon after, Rome, not Florence, would be the headquarters of the next great artistic movement: baroque.

LATE RENAISSANCE AND MANNERISM

In reaction to the rigid pursuit of harmony and naturalism of the Renaissance, a new generation of artists, working from about 1520 to 1580, founded the mannerist school. Andrea del Sarto (1486–1531), who painted the Chiostro dello Scalzo (p86), and especially Pontormo (1494–1557), whose greatest work is found in the Chiesa di Santa Felicità (p109), deliberately distorted forms and perspective and relied on a palette of exaggerated, even unnatural colours. Michelangelo's quietly disturbing Biblioteca Medicea-Laurenziana (p76) and Cappelle Medicee (p77) are also considered defining works of mannerism. Ironically, Giorgio Vasari (1511–74), the man who coined the term 'Renaissance' (p64) and whose theories defined generations of art history, is himself considered mannerist. He was also the last of the city's great artists, though his architecture and writings outstrip his paintings. Fittingly, his Palazzo degli Uffizi serves as the repository of the phenomenon he himself named.

DIRECTORY
TRANSPORT

Florence has international train and bus stations in the city centre and offers easy connections to nearby airports. Driving into the city is not recommended because of traffic and parking. If you do drive in, ensure that you register your car with the hotel where you are staying. If you are not staying in a hotel, you cannot drive in the city centre and risk getting a hefty fine. The main parts of interest in the city can be reached fairly easily on foot.

ARRIVAL & DEPARTURE
AIR
Aeroporto di Firenze

Aeroporto di Firenze (Florence Airport; ☎ 055 30 61 300; www.aeroporto.firenze.it), 5km northwest of the city centre, serves domestic and a growing number of European flights. **SITAbus** (www.sitabus.it, in Italian) operates buses between Florence Airport (€4.50, 20 minutes, every 30 minutes between 6am and 11pm) and the SITA bus station (Map pp60–1, F2) in central Florence. Taxis charge a fixed fee of €16 from the airport to addresses in central Florence.

Pisa International Airport Galileo Galilei

Pisa International Airport Galileo Galilei (☎ 050 84 93 00; www.pisa-airport.com) is substantially larger than Florence Airport and one of northern Italy's main international and domestic airports. It is located about 1km outside Pisa and about 90km west of Florence. It is well linked to Florence by public transport. **Terravision** (www.terravision.eu; single/return €8/16; 1¼ hours, from Florence 12 daily 3.30am-7pm, from Pisa hourly 8.30am-midnight) coaches shuttle passengers between the bus stop outside Florence's Stazione di Santa Maria

Novella on Via Luigi Alamanni (Map pp60–1, F2) and Pisa International Airport Galileo Galilei. In Florence tickets are sold at the Hotel Reservations Office inside the train station and at the Terravision desk inside **Deanna Bar** (Via Luigi Alamanni 9r; ☺ 6am-7pm) opposite the Terravision bus stop. At Pisa airport, the Terravision ticket desk dominates the arrival hall. You can also reserve seats and purchase tickets online. Equally comfortable, cheaper (and more reliable in the early morning when coach timetables have been known to change at the last minute) are the regular trains that link Florence's Stazione di Santa Maria Novella with Pisa International Airport Galileo Galilei (€5.20, 1½ hours, at least hourly from 6.30am to 5pm).

TRAIN
Florence's central train station **Stazione di Santa Maria Novella** (Piazza della Stazione) has regional, national and international services (www .trenitalia.com). There are direct services to many European cities. Reliable and self-explanatory touch-screen machines provide speed ticketing. Florence is on the Rome–Milan line, with fast, frequent express service to/from Rome, Bologna, Milan and Venice. Very frequent regional trains also run to Lucca, Pisa and Siena.

THE RED & THE BLACK
Florence has two parallel systems for street-numbering: red or brown numbers (which usually have 'r' for *rosso*, or red, after the number) indicate commercial premises; black or blue ones are for private residences.

Black/blue numbers may denote whole buildings, while each red/brown number refers to one commercial entity – and a building may have several. It can turn you purple if you're hunting in a hurry for a specific address.

BUS
Lazzi (Map pp60–1, G1; ☎ 055 21 51 55; www .lazzi.it, in Italian; Piazza della Stazione) is located just outside Stazione di Santa Maria Novella and forms part of the Eurolines network of international bus services with services to a large network of European cities.

GETTING AROUND
By far the easiest way to get around Florence is by foot. This is also a great way to acquaint yourself with the city's neighbourhoods. All major sights are within a leisurely 20-minute walk from one another – almost always quicker than taking city buses or even taxis in the gridlocked centre. The Tramvia is not likely to be completed before publication. In any case the line that is somewhat near completion is definitely not useful to tourists.

BUS

ATAF (Azienda Transport Area Fiorentina; ☎ 800 424 500; www.ataf.net) buses and electric *bussini* (minibuses) serve the city and its periphery. Most lines start/terminate at the ATAF bus stops (Map pp60–1, G1) opposite the southeastern exit of Stazione di Santa Maria Novella. Tickets cost €1.20 (€2 on board) and are good for 70 minutes on any bus. They are sold at newspaper kiosks, tobacconists and the ATAF **ticket & information office** (Piazza Adua; ☽ 7am-8pm), next to the bus stops opposite Stazione di Santa Maria Novella. You can also buy a book of 10/21 tickets for €10/20. Don't forget to validate your ticket in the time-stamp machine inside the bus or risk paying a fine upwards of €40. Handy lines include 36, 37 and 11 (connecting Stazione di Santa Maria Novella and the Oltrarno), 12 and 13 (connecting Stazione di Santa Maria Novella and San Miniato al Monte) and 23 and 14 (connecting Stazione di Santa Maria Novella and Santa Croce).

BICYCLE

Cycling is a great way to get around the city, though remember you're in Italy, so don't expect drivers to yield every time. Exercise caution even in the city's small but growing number of bike lanes. For a longer ride, the Il Chianti country-side (p144) makes for excellent cycling. Florence has some companies that organise bicycle tours (p180). Bike rentals run around €12 to €14 per day and €50 to €60 per week. Two options to check out:
Alinari (Map pp74-5, D4; ☎ 055 280 500; www.alinarirental.com; Via San Zanobi 38r)
Florence by Bike (Map pp74-5, E2; ☎ 055 488 992; www.florencebybike.it; Via San Zanobi 120r)

CAR

Only residents and hotel guests have the right to drive in central Florence, a rule enforced by cameras. Fines are upwards of €100. If you drive into the centre, make sure your hotel registers your license plate number with local police.

TAXI

Taxi rides within the city centre cost less than €10. Hailing a taxi is difficult and you won't find taxi stands. If you need a taxi, it's best to ring for one.
Radio Taxi Firenze (☎ 055 43 90)
Socota (☎ 055 42 42, 055 47 98)

PRACTICALITIES
BUSINESS HOURS

Banks and public offices 8.30am to 1.30pm and 3pm to 5pm Monday to Friday
Post offices 8.30am to 1pm Monday to Friday; some reopen 3pm to 5pm
Restaurants lunch from noon to 3pm, dinner from 7.30pm to 10pm
Shops 10am to 1pm and 4pm to 7pm Monday to Friday and 10am to 1pm Saturday

DISCOUNTS

Almost all museums and most churches offer discounts of 30% to 50% for European Union residents aged over 65 years and under 26 years. You must present a valid picture ID.

ELECTRICITY

Electricity is 220V. Most plugs accept two-pin, European-style plugs. Some also accommodate American-style plugs. Adapters and transformers can be purchased at stores called either *elettricità* (electrical) or *ferramenta* (hardware).

HOLIDAYS

New Year's Day (Anno Nuovo) 1 January
Epiphany (Befana) 6 January
Easter Sunday (Pasqua) March or April
Easter Monday (Pasquetta) March or April
Liberation Day (Festa della Liberazione) 25 April – marks the Allied victory in Italy in WWII
Labour Day (Festa del Lavoro) 1 May
Foundation of the Italian Republic (Festa della Repubblica) 2 June
Assumption Day (Ferragosto) 15 August
All Saints' Day (Ognissanti) 1 November
Day of the Immaculate Conception (Concezione Immaculata) 8 December
Christmas (Natale) 25 December
St Stephen's Day/Boxing Day (Festa di Santo Stefano) 26 December

INTERNET

While technically there is free, public wi-fi access in central Florence, service is spotty and connections often very slow when you can get them. However, most hotels and an increasing number of cafes offer wi-fi service. Internet cafes are abundant and can be found throughout the city centre. Prices run around €5 per hour. Note that internet cafes require a photo ID due to a much-ridiculed Italian anti-terrorism law. Some useful websites can be found, below.

INTERNET RESOURCES & ORGANISATIONS

British Institute of Florence (www.british institute.it) Offers excellent art history and Italian language classes as well as regular cultural events.
Firenze Spettacolo (www.firenzespettacolo .it, in Italian) Definitive nightlife and events listings.
Lonely Planet (www.lonelyplanet.com)
Made in Tuscany Magazine (www.firenze magazine.it) Insight into who's who in Florence's cultural scene as well as fashion, food and wine reviews.
Tuscan Tourist Board (www.turismo.toscana .it) Provides ideas for tailored itineraries in Florence and around Tuscany.
Studentsville (www.studentsville.it) Everything about studying, living and lodging in this student-busy city.
The Florentine (www.theflorentine.it) Local English-language newspaper with news and reviews of cultural events.

LANGUAGE

The Tuscan dialect forms the basis of the Italian language. Ironically, though, Tuscans are generally harder to understand than others speaking standard Italian, because they tend to pronounce the hard 'c' sound as 'h', particularly at the beginning of a word. For example 'casa' (house) would be pronounced 'hasa'.

BASICS

Hello.	*Buongiorno.*
Hi/bye.	*Ciao.*
Goodbye.	*Arrivederci.*
Please.	*Per favore.*
Thanks.	*Grazie.*
How are you?	*Come sta?*
I'm fine, thanks.	*Bene, grazie.*
Excuse me.	*Mi scusi/Permesso.*
You're welcome.	*Prego.*
Yes/No.	*Sì/No.*
How much?	*Quanto costa?*
That's too expensive.	*È troppo caro.*
Do you speak English?	*Parla inglese?*
I don't understand.	*Non capisco.*
Two beers please?	*Due birre, per favore.*
Where is...?	*Dove...?*
What time is it?	*Que ore sono?*

EATING & DRINKING

That was delicious!	*Era squisito!*
I'm a vegetarian.	*Sono vegetariano/a.* (m/f)
Please bring the bill.	*Il conto, per favore.*

EMERGENCIES

I'm sick.	*Sono ammalato/a.* (m/f)
Help!	*Aiuto!*
Call the police.	*Chiami la polizia!*
Call an ambulance.	*Chiami un'ambulanza!*

MONEY

The euro has been the official currency of Italy since it was launched in 2002. One euro is divided into 100 cents or *centimi*. Notes come in denominations of five, 10, 20, 50, 100 and 500 euros. See the inside front cover for approximate exchange rates or consult current rates at www.xe.com.

COSTS

Experienced budget travellers can get away with spending €50 a day on top of accommodation, including two budget meals, a snack and coffee, a couple of museums and an evening *aperitivo* (p56). Upgrade to a couple of gourmet dinners and a night on the town and expect to spend about €80 to €100.

ORGANISED TOURS

Bicycle Tuscany (☎ 055 22 25 80; www .bicycletuscany.com; ⏰ Mar–Nov) One-day bike rides in the Tuscan countryside (€60 incl transport, bike and equipment, lunch and winery visit).

Florence Guided Tours (Map pp42-3, E4; ☎ 055 210 301, 349 316 46 77; www.flora promotuscany.com; Via della Condotta 12) Florence in a Day (€70), the Uffizi (€30), Galleria dell'Accademia (€25) and various theme tours.

I Bike Tuscany (☎ 335 8120 769; www.ibike tuscany.com; Via Belgio 4) One-day rides on the outskirts of Florence, Siena & Il Chianti led by former bike racer Marco Vignoli. It's located a long way southeast of the centre.

Mercurio Tours (Map pp74-5, E6; ☎ 055 213 355; www.mercurio-italy.org; Via Cavour 8) Three-hour walking tours of the city (€42.50) & half-day Chianti trips (€67.50). Reserve by phone or in person at Amici del Turismo (Map pp74-5, E6; Via Cavour 36r).

The Original & Best Walking Tours of Florence (Map pp42-3, B4; ☎ 055 264 50 33, 329 613 27 30; www.italy.artviva.com; Via dei Sassetti 1) Excellent one- to three-hour walks of the city (€25 to €39) led by historians or art history graduates, including an evening Medici murder stroll (€25, 1½ hours).

....

TELEPHONE

Italy uses the GSM 900/1800 mobile (cell) phone system, compatible with phones from the UK, Europe, Australia and most of Asia, and dual-band GSM 1900/900 phones from North America and Japan. Public phones are plentiful in Florence, although most only accept *schede telefoniche* (phone cards). Cards cost €5, €10 and €20 and can be bought from *tabacchi*, as well as some newsstands and bars. For international calls, it's better value to buy one of a range of long-distance phone cards from *tabacchi*.

COUNTRY & CITY CODES

Florence city code	☎ 055
Country code	☎ 39

USEFUL PHONE NUMBERS

Directory assistance	☎ 12
International access code	☎ 00

Local taxi	☎ 055 43 90
Medical emergency	☎ 111 83 94
Tourist police	☎ 055 203 911

....

TIPPING

Service is almost always included in the price of your meal. If service was particularly good, you can always leave another euro or two, but this is not at all mandatory. In restaurants where service is not included, it's customary to leave a 10% tip. Rounding your taxi fare to the nearest euro will suffice, and don't forget to drop about €2 to €4 into the porter's hand at A-list hotels.

....

TOURIST INFORMATION

Comune di Firenze Tourist Office Train Station (Map pp60–1, G2; ☎ 055 21 22 45; www .comune.fi.it, in Italian; Piazza della Stazione 4; 8.30am-7pm Mon-Sat, 8.30am-1.30pm Sun); Santa Croce (Map p95, B3; ☎ 055 234 04 44; Borgo Santa Croce 29r; 9am-7pm Mon-Sat, 9am-2pm Sun) Information on the city, run by Florence's city council.

Provincia di Firenze Tourist Office City Centre (Map pp74-5, E6; ☎ 055 29 08 32/3; www.provincia.firenze.it, in Italian; www .firenzeturismo.it; Via Cavour 1r; 8.30am-6.30pm Mon-Sat, 8.30am-1.30pm Sun); Florence Airport (☎ 055 31 58 74; infoaero porto@aeroporto.firenze.it; 8.30am-8.30pm) Information on the city and province of Florence: stocks lists of recommended guided tours, updated museum opening hours and accommodation; sells books and maps. Also runs the **SOS Turista phoneline** (☎ 055 276 03 82) for tourists in trouble (disputes over hotel bills etc).

DIRECTORY

TRAVELLERS WITH DISABILITIES

While there have been improvements in recent years, services and infrastructure for people with disabilities in and around Florence still leave something to be desired. Tiny lifts, unruly traffic and cobbled streets can make circulating through the city a challenge. That said, improvements are being made: newer buses can generally accommodate wheelchairs and most museums now have ramps. An excellent resource is the non-profit **Accessible Italy** (www.accessible italy.com), which provides a list of suitable accommodation and a list of accessible sights. It also organizes both small group tours and independent travel for travellers with physical of visual disabilities.

Portrait of Equerry
Giorgione

>INDEX

See also separate subindexes for See (p189), Shop (p190), Eat (p191), Drink (p192) and Play (p192).

000 map pages

INDEX

000 map pages